BUILDING DEFECTS

Adam Constable

and

Calum Lamont

RICS BOOKS

Acknowledgements

Crown copyright material is reproduced with the permission of the Controller of HMSO and the Queen's Printer for Scotland.

Clauses from the *ICE Conditions of Contract* (7th edition) are reproduced with permission, Institution of Civil Engineers.

Clauses from contracts by the Joint Contracts Tribunal Limited, Sweet & Maxwell, © The Joint Contracts Tribunal Limited, are reproduced here with permission.

Clauses from the *NEC3 Engineering and Construction Contract* are reproduced here with permission from NEC Contracts.

Clause 7.3 from the *Standard Form of Agreement for the Appointment of an Architect* (SFA/1999) is reproduced here with permission from RIBA Enterprises.

Please note: References to the masculine include, where appropriate, the feminine.

Published by RICS Business Services Limited
a wholly owned subsidiary of
The Royal Institution of Chartered Surveyors
under the RICS Books imprint
Surveyor Court
Westwood Business Park
Coventry CV4 8JE
UK
www.ricsbooks.com

ISBN 978 1 84219 294 9

ISBN 1 84219 294 9 (prior to January 2007)

Typeset in Great Britain by Columns Design Ltd, Reading, Berks

Printed in Great Britain by Bell & Bain, Glasgow

Contents

Contents

Preface

While chartered surveyors may not need the *breadth* of understanding of the law of their opposite numbers in the legal profession, in a number of key areas of application to construction and property they need a similar *depth* of knowledge. Exactly what the key areas may be depends to some extent on the nature of the surveyor's practice. There are plenty of building surveyors, for example, who know more about the law relating to Party Walls and plenty of quantity surveyors who know more about construction adjudications, than the average lawyer in general practice.

So surveyors need law and, for a variety of reasons, need to maintain and develop their understanding of it. Changing trends or individual variations in clients' requirements mean that from time to time even the best practitioners (perhaps especially the best practitioners) will feel the need to expand their legal knowledge. The knowledge acquired at college, or in studying for the RICS Assessment of Professional Competence ('APC'), has a limited shelf-life and needs to be constantly updated to maintain its currency. Even specialists working in their areas of expertise need a source of reference as an aide-mémoire or as a first port of call in more detailed research.

The Case in Point series

RICS Books is committed to meeting the needs of surveying (and other) professionals and the Case in Point series typifies that commitment. It is aimed at those who need to upgrade or update their legal knowledge or who need to have access to a good first reference at the outset of an inquiry. A particular difficulty is the burgeoning of reported decisions of the courts. The sheer scale of the law reports, both general and specialist, makes it very hard even to be aware of recent trends, let alone identify the significance of a particular decision. Thus it was decided to focus on developments in case law. In any given matter, the practitioner will want to be directed efficiently and painlessly to the decision that bears upon the matter he or she is dealing with, in other words to 'the case in point'. The books in the Case in Point series offer a wealth of legal information which is essential in its practical application to the work of the surveyor or other construction professional. The authors have the level of expertise required to be selective and succinct, thus achieving a high degree of relevance without sacrificing accessibility. The series has developed incrementally and now forms a collection of specialist handbooks which can deliver what practitioners need – the law on the matter they are handling, when they want it.

Building Defects by Adam Constable and Calum Lamont

Defects will occur in buildings. It is one of the great certainties in construction, the equivalent of death and taxes in life more generally. This is not to suggest that all attempts at prevention are useless and should give way to fatalism. Better design and construction teams produce better work, and efficient management and quality control can reduce the incidence of defects very considerably. But no construction industry in the world can claim to have achieved perfection; the human element in the process is enough to ensure that. So defects will occur.

Given that they will occur, it is a necessary function of the law to deal with the consequences, to regulate the rights and responsibilities of the participants in the project, whether it be new build, refurbishment or the acquisition of a building. Put simply, the question can often be reduced to two words – who pays?

In many cases, the answer will be provided, at least in part, by the provisions of the construction contract. Some contracts define defects and set up procedures for their rectification and allocation of responsibility for financial consequences.

However, it would be a gross over-simplification to suggest that reference to the contract provides all the answers. Not all contracts define defects and not all provide for the consequences. Whether an apparent disconformity during or after construction can be classified as a defect may be a highly contentious question. The parties may have agreed a defects liability period, but how does that operate in relation to the rules on limitation of action? Away from new-build, a surveyor carrying out an inspection of a building will want to know his or her responsibilities for the observation and interpretation of defects in reporting to the client and the consequences of failure to do so.

These are legal questions and statute law provides at best partial help in answering them. The *Defective Premises Act* is, of course, only concerned with dwellings, while it would not be unfair to say that the *Limitation Act* and the *Latent Damage Act* have generated controversies in trying to resolve them.

Thus it is that a body of case law has grown up as the courts have tried to answer these and other crucial questions.

In marshalling this case law, the authors have dealt with both contractual and tortious rights of action for defective work. They devote a chapter to cases on the 'temporary disconformity theory' and another to judicial interpretations of the *Defective Premises Act*. Crucially for general practitioners, whether in valuation or building surveying, there is a chapter on the surveyor's duty to identify defects. The sheer complexity of the limitation rules is tackled through the cases and there is useful guidance on remedies.

The collection and analysis of the case law in this disciplined and practical way has demanded an exceptional team. The authors are both barristers at Keating Chambers, a leading set in construction-related work. Adam Constable has more than ten years' experience of major construction litigation and arbitration, including a number of appearances in the Court of Appeal; he was appointed as Treasury Counsel in 2004. He publishes frequently in legal and industry journals.

Calum Lamont was called to the Bar in 2004 after a Double First at Cambridge. He has advised in a number of significant construction disputes and recently appeared in the Technology and Construction Court in *All in One Building v Makers UK* [2006] CILL 2321.

Together, the authors have produced a sharply-focussed account of the case law on defects, a welcome addition to the construction Case in Point titles, which include Adjudication and Party Walls.

Anthony Lavers, 2006.
Professional Support Lawyer, White & Case, London.
Visiting Professor of Law, Oxford Brookes University.
Consultant Editor, Case in Point series.

Introduction

All manner of disputes and disagreements arise out of defective work. The most basic question will be whether a defect exists. Sometimes the answer to this will be obvious, but where the specification for work is complex it may be a matter for fine technical judgment as to whether the work carried out is defective. Whilst the parties may be concerned with defects they can see, often difficult problems arise by reason of defects that are not immediately observable. The first chapter of this book considers what constitutes a defect, and explains what makes a defect either 'patent' or 'latent'.

Where the parties' relationship is governed by a contract, it is usually this which will underlie what in any given situation may constitute defective work. However, in modern building practice the contract will also usually be important in providing a mechanism by which defects can be dealt with, either as they arise during the construction project or after the conclusion of the work. Standard defects liability provisions are considered in Chapter 2, together with the effect of these clauses upon other rights or liabilities the parties may have.

Chapter 3 is concerned with the concept of 'temporary disconformity', and the question of whether or to what extent a builder might be liable for defects during the course of the works. If the builder is putting the defects right (or is capable of doing so), does the employer have any recourse?

Chapters 4 and 5 go on to consider the rights and remedies available for defective work outside of a contract. Whether it is a subsequent purchaser saddled with a defective property, an employer seeking to sue a sub-contractor for defective work in circumstances where the contractor is insolvent, or a party whose claim in contract is statute-barred, circumstances arise where a claim for defects must be brought in tort. Complex questions arise as to the nature of the defect and the damage caused where a claim is brought for negligence. This is because, ordinarily, a party does not owe another party a duty of care at common law to prevent loss which is 'purely economic' and does not arise out of some physical damage or injury. These principles, and the exceptions to them, are explored in Chapter 4. If a party cannot bring its claim for defects in tort, it might be able to rely upon statute. In Chapter 5, claims under the *Defective Premises Act* 1972 are considered.

The identification of defects when a purchaser buys a property is often key. If a significant defect is not spotted, the purchaser will pay over the odds. Almost all property transactions are nowadays subject to a survey, not least because mortgage lenders require a valuation. The obligation upon surveyors to identify defects, the nature of inspections, and the type of situations in which the surveyor will be held responsible for failing to identify defects are dealt with in Chapter 6.

Limitation of actions is an area which brings together a number of themes relevant to defective works. Whether a defect is patent or latent will impact upon the discoverability, and indeed discovery, of a defect. How does the law deal with the emergence of defects many years after the work has been designed and constructed? Moreover, parties are often forced to find ingenious ways of characterising their defects claim – in terms of the losses caused – in order to avoid the impact of the *Limitation Act* 1980. These matters are the subject of Chapter 7.

In the penultimate chapter, we explore how defects affect the responsibilities of the project team, and the nature of construction professionals' obligations in relation to either their own defective work or that of other people.

Finally, in Chapter 9, the question of how to assess loss arising from defective work is dealt with. Specifically, Chapter 9 considers the approaches through which courts decide whether to award the affected party the cost of effecting repairs, the diminution in value to the property or chattel caused by the defects, or damages calculated on some other basis. Questions of betterment, mitigation and consequential losses, including claims for distress and inconvenience, are also the subject of this chapter.

List of Acts, Statutory Instruments and abbreviations

The following Acts and Statutory Instruments are referenced in this publication. Where a piece of legislation is mentioned frequently, it is referred to by the abbreviation that follows the name of the legislation in brackets.

Civil Liability (Contribution) Act 1978
Defective Premises Act 1972 **('DPA 1972')**
Employers' Liability Act 1880
Housing Act 1985
Housing Act 2004
Landlord and Tenant Act 1985
Latent Damage Act 1986
Limitation Act 1939
Limitation Act 1980
London Building Act 1894

Civil Procedure Rules 1998, SI 1998/3132

The text of this publication is divided into commentary and case summaries. The commentary is enclosed between grey highlighted lines for ease of reference.

Table of cases

1
What is a 'defect'?

There have been various attempts at defining a 'defect'. Absent a specific definition with any particular contract, it is necessary to consider what might constitute a 'defect' and, furthermore, when a defect is 'latent' or 'patent'. Whilst a number of the early authorities relate to the existence of 'defects' in plant or machinery, in the context of employers' liability, they serve as useful guidance as to the breadth of the definition of a 'defect'.

1.1 MEANING OF DEFECT

Tate v Latham (1897)

The plaintiff was employed at the defendants' saw-mills to assist one of their sawyers who was engaged at a circular saw. The issue was whether the absence of the guard was a defect in the condition of the machinery within s. 1(1) of the *Employers' Liability Act* 1880. It was held that 'defect' means a lack or absence of something essential to completeness. The machinery or plant in question was a bench or table supporting a circular saw. The saw revolved in a slit in the bench, part of the disc of the saw being above the table and part below. It followed from a finding that it was necessary to the completeness of the machinery or plant to have a plank or shutter fitted to the side of the table as a screen or fence to protect persons working near the saw-bench from the part of the saw which was under the bench that its absence constituted a 'defect'. A machine may be in its nature and character a perfect machine and may yet be in an imperfect and defective condition.

Yarmouth v France (1887)

It was the plaintiff's job to drive carts and to load and unload the goods that were carried in them. One of the cart horses was vicious and unfit to be driven even by a careful driver. The plaintiff objected to driving this horse, and told the foreman of the stable that the horse was unfit to be driven, to which the foreman replied that the plaintiff must go on driving it, and that if any accident happened his employer would be responsible. The plaintiff was injured in an accident whilst driving the cart. Having first considered that the horse could constitute 'plant' for the purposes of the relevant statute, Lindley LJ went on to consider whether vice in a horse can be a defect in the condition of plant. He stated that a defect included 'anything which renders the plant, etc. unfit for the use for which it is intended, when used in a reasonable way and with reasonable care'.

Jackson v Mumford (1904)

It was held by the Court of Appeal that a 'latent defect in the machinery' could not cover a weakness of design. Kennedy J held in the context of a claim under marine insurance that,

> 'It is not a natural interpretation of the words … The phrase "defect in machinery" in a business document means a defect of material, in respect either of its original composition or in respect of its after acquired conditions …'

This is perhaps a surprising conclusion, and may be confined to its facts. Generally, a product that is incapable of performing its intended task would be considered to be defective, whether the cause of its defective state is the design, materials or a combination of the two.

Robertson v Kinneil Cannel & Coking Coal Co (1932)

In this case it was found that a 'defect in the condition of the ways, works, machinery or plant' of the employer refers to a defect in good working condition and is not confined to the presence of the physical parts of the machinery or plant.

Barry v Minturn (1913)

Dampness in a party wall was not a defect within the meaning of s. 88 of the *London Building Act* 1894, unless it rendered the wall less effective for the purposes for which it was used or intended to be used.

1.2 'DEFECTS' DEFINED BY REFERENCE TO OTHER TERMS

It may well be that a contract defines expressly what a 'defect' is (see, for example, the NEC 3rd edition at 2.8 below). Even if it does not, the terms of the contract will shape what may or may not constitute a defect. For example, a contract to build a wall which is silent as to the use of a particular sort of brick may be satisfied providing the materials and workmanship used are of satisfactory quality. However, if the contractor builds a perfectly adequate wall with red brick, but the contract specifies the use of yellow London Stock, the wall may nevertheless be considered 'defective'. It is the lack of compliance with the specification rather than any inherent problem with the quality of workmanship or materials which renders the wall defective.

For this reason, the existence of a defect is closely related to the obligations of the contractor. In a simple contract, where there is a limited or unsophisticated specification, this may well depend upon the implication of a term.

Lynch v Thorne (1956)

The plaintiff contracted with a builder for the construction of a house to live in. It was held that there is an implied condition that the house, when built, shall be fit for human habitation, subject to any express terms of the contract which may be such as to show that they are wholly or partly inconsistent with any such implied condition. If wholly inconsistent, that will clearly negate any reliance which otherwise it would be said the buyer placed on the skill and judgment of the builder. If, on the other hand, the express terms are only partly inconsistent, there will be room for the implied condition to operate in the area not covered by the express condition.

Hancock v Brazier (1966)

This claim concerned whether a contractor was liable to a plaintiff when the floor failed by reason of sodium sulphates within the hardcore base. It was held that the formulation of the implied warranty is sometimes varied by the use of the words 'a house fit for human habitation', but

'... there is no substantial or significant difference between the formulation of the warranty that the house should be built of materials suitable and fit and proper for the purpose and the work should be carried out in a proper, efficient and workmanlike manner, and the alternative way of stating it, that the house is habitable and fit for humans to live in'.

It should be noted that in *Hancock*, on the evidence, a case of negligence against the builder had not been made out. This is because although it was known in 1959 that soluble sulphates were capable of attacking hardcore, the danger was not one which was generally recognised as likely to arise in the ordinary course of building a house and acquiring hardcore for it.

Thus, a failure to provide proper materials is likely to give rise to the existence of a 'defect', irrespective of the question of negligence. Whether that defect is 'patent' or 'latent' is considered further below. Liability for latent defects is considered further in later chapters of this book.

1.3   WHEN IS A DEFECT 'PATENT' AND WHEN IS IT 'LATENT'?

It is often important to distinguish between patent and latent defects. It may be that a contract has specific mechanisms for defects becoming patent during a certain period (e.g. a defects liability period: see Chapter 2) whereas latent defects are dealt with otherwise. Alternatively, a surveyor may well be under a duty to identify patent defects in a property whereas latent defects would not, self evidently, be something which the surveyor could be expected to spot.

Yandle & Sons v Sutton, Young and Sutton (1922)

The issue for the court was whether, in the context of the sale of land, a right of way across the land was a latent or a patent defect. In considering what is a latent defect and what is a patent defect, the court took the general view, that a patent defect must be a defect which arises either to the eye, or by necessary implication from something which is visible to the eye.

Sanderson v National Coal Board (1961)

A miner working by only his cap light in a confined space beside a moving conveyor was injured when one or more of the conveyor belt hooks came adrift and lacerated his leg. The trial judge held that the plaintiff had failed to prove that the defect in the belt existed for four or five minutes before he was injured; therefore, the National Coal Board had proved that it was impracticable for them to avoid or prevent the admitted contravention. It was held that:

> 'A patent defect is not latent when there is none to observe it. The natural meaning of the word "patent" is objective, not subjective. It means "observable", not "observed". A patent defect must be apparent on inspection, but it is not dependent on the eye of the observer; it can blush unseen. In this case, although the defect was in darkness, it was patent. Had the plaintiff or his mate shone their lamps on it at the relevant moment, they would have seen it. The construction of the word "patent" for which the defendants contend involves the conclusion that a patent defect at the belt head becomes a latent defect immediately it has turned over the rollers and is making its hidden journey in the darkness, and that it is intermittently latent or patent according to its position. Such a construction is unreasonable ...'

Riverstone Meat Co Pty Ltd v Lancashire Shipping Company Ltd (1961)

Latent defects, in the strict sense, include defects making for unseaworthiness in the ship, however caused, if these could not be discovered by the purchaser, or competent experts employed by him, by the exercise of due diligence.

(1) Baxall Securities Ltd (2) Norbain Sdc Ltd v (1) Sheard Walshaw Partnership (2) Shaw Whitmore Partnership (3) Birse Construction Ltd (4) Fk Roofing Ltd (5) Fullflow Ltd (2002)

> 'The concept of a latent defect is not a difficult one. It means a concealed flaw. What is a flaw? It is the actual defect in the workmanship or design, not the danger presented by the defect.'

There is, accordingly, a question of degree. The consumer of a fizzy drink will not, in the normal course, bring in an expert to inspect the goods he purchased. In marked contrast, the buyer of a building almost invariably would. Certainly in the commercial context, a defect would not be latent if it had been reasonably discoverable by the claimant with the benefit of such skilled third party advice as he might be expected to retain.

1.4 SUMMARY

From these cases it can be concluded that:

- Whether a defect is latent or patent is to be determined *objectively*. The fact that a defect was not *in fact* identified may therefore be of some evidential value but is not of itself determinative of the question of whether, at any particular time, a defect was latent or patent.

- A patent defect can include those matters which are the necessary consequence of something observable.

- Whether a defect is 'latent' will depend upon the extent of inspection to which the product is ordinarily – or in fact – subjected.

2
Defects liability and other contractual provisions

2.1 INTRODUCTION

It is commonplace in standard form contracts that there are included 'defects liability' provisions. Usually, the liability commences at the completion of the works (variously defined as 'practical completion' or 'substantial completion', or similar), and lasts for a defined period agreed between the parties. The clause will impose obligations upon the contractor to make good defects, but those obligations will usually also be counterbalanced by the *right* to make good defects. This would ordinarily be to the contractor's advantage given this is likely to be less costly than providing an indemnity to the employer against the cost of having another contractor fix the defective work.

Moreover, other contractual provisions can impact upon the nature and extent of a contractor's liability for defects.

This chapter provides an overview of common forms of defects liability provisions and considers the principles arising out of them.

2.2 JCT STANDARD FORMS

Joint Contract Tribunal Standard Form of Building Contract (1998 edition)

'Clause 17

17.1 When in the opinion of the Architect/the Contract Administrator Practical Completion of the Works is achieved and the Contractor has complied sufficiently with clause 6A.4, and, if relevant, the Contractor has complied with clause 5.9 (*Supply* of as-built drawings, etc. – Performance Specified Work), he shall forthwith issue a certificate to that effect and Practical Completion of the Works shall be deemed for all the purposes of this Contract to have taken place on the day named in such certificate.

17.2 Any defects, shrinkages or other faults which shall appear within the Defects Liability Period and which are due to materials or workmanship not in accordance with this Contract or to frost occurring before Practical Completion of the Works, shall be specified by the Architect/the Contract Administrator in a schedule of defects which he shall deliver to the Contractor as an instruction of the Architect/the Contract Administrator not later than 14 days after the expiration of the said Defects Liability Period, and within a reasonable time after receipt of such schedule the defects, shrinkages and other faults therein specified shall be made good by the Contractor at no cost to the Employer unless the Architect/the Contract Administrator with the consent of the Employer shall otherwise instruct; and if the Architect/the Contract Administrator does so otherwise instruct then an appropriate deduction in respect of any such defects, shrinkages or other faults not made good shall be made from the Contract Sum.

17.3 Notwithstanding clause 17.2 the Architect/the Contract Administrator may whenever he considers it necessary so to do, issue instructions requiring any defect, shrinkage or other fault which shall appear within the Defects Liability Period and which is due to materials or workmanship not in accordance with this Contract or to frost occurring before Practical Completion of the Works, to be made good, and the Contractor shall within a reasonable time after receipt of such instructions comply with the same at no cost to the Employer unless the Architect/the Contract Administrator with the consent of the Employer shall otherwise instruct; and if the Architect/the Contract Administrator does so otherwise instruct then an appropriate deduction in respect of any such defects, shrinkages or other faults not made good shall be made from the Contract Sum. Provided that no such instructions shall be issued after delivery of a schedule of defects or after 14 days from the expiration of the Defects Liability Period.

17.4 When in the opinion of the Architect/the Contract Administrator any defects, shrinkages or other faults which he may have required to be made good under clause 17.2 and 17.3 shall have been made good he shall issue a certificate to that effect, and completion of making good defects shall be deemed for all the purposes of this Contract to have taken place on the day named in such certificate (the "Certificate of Completion of Making Good Defects").

17.5 In no case shall the Contractor be required to make good at his own cost any damage by frost which may appear after Practical Completion, unless the Architect/the Contract Administrator shall certify that such damage is due to injury which took place before Practical Completion.'

Clause 17 from the Standard Form of Building Contract (1998 edition), © the Joint Contracts Tribunal Limited 1998, publisher Sweet & Maxwell, is reproduced here with permission.

See, however, that in the 2005 suite of JCT contracts the 'Defects Liability Period' has been replaced by what is now called a 'Rectification Period'. The principle remains the same, but the wording has been somewhat simplified. For example, see clauses 2.35 and 2.36 within the JCT *Design and Build Standard Form of Contract 2005*:

'JCT Design and Build Standard Form of Contract 2005

2.35 If any defects, shrinkages or other faults in the Works or a Section appear within the relevant Rectification Period due to any failure of the Contractor to comply with his obligations under this Contract:

> 1 such defects, shrinkages and other faults shall be specified by the Employer in a schedule of defects which he shall deliver to the Contractor as an instruction not later than 14 days after the expiry of that Rectification Period; and

> 2 notwithstanding clause 2.35.1, the Employer may whenever he considers it necessary issue instructions requiring any such defect, shrinkage or other fault to be made good, provided no instructions under this clause 2.35.2 shall be issued after delivery of a schedule of defects or more than 14 days after the expiry of the relevant Rectification Period.

Within a reasonable time after receipt of such schedule or instructions, the defects, shrinkages and other faults shall at no cost to the Employer be made good by the Contractor unless the Employer shall otherwise instruct. If he does so otherwise instruct, an appropriate deduction shall be made from the Contract sum in respect of the defects, shrinkages or other faults not made good.

2.36 When the defects, shrinkages or other faults in the Works or a Section which the Employer has required to be made good under clause 2.35 have been made good, he shall issue a notice to that effect (a "Notice of Completion of Making Good"), which notice shall not be unreasonably delayed or withheld, and completion of that making good shall for the purposes of this Contract be deemed to have taken place on the date stated in that notice.'

Clauses 2.35 and 2.36 from the Design and Build Standard Form of Contract 2005, © the Joint Contracts Tribunal Limited 2005, publisher Sweet & Maxwell, are reproduced here with permission.

The JCT *Minor Works Contract* (for example, 1998 edition) also retains the basic concept of a defects liability period, but expresses the rights and obligations in short and simple form (see *William Tomkinson v St Michael's PCC* at 2.10 below):

'2.5 Any defects, excessive shrinkages or other faults to the Works which appear within [three months] of the date of practical completion and are due to materials or workmanship not in accordance with this Agreement or frost occurring before practical completion shall be made good by the Contractor entirely at his own cost unless the Architect/the Contract Administrator shall otherwise instruct. The Architect/The Contract Administrator shall certify the date when in his opinion the Contractor's obligations under this Clause 2.5 have been discharged.'

Clause 2.5 from the JCT Minor Works Contract (1998 edition), © the Joint Contracts Tribunal Limited 1998, publisher Sweet & Maxwell, is reproduced here with permission.

Note some subtle differences, however, in the wording of the clause to the *Standard Form* and *Design and Build Forms*. In particular, a defect or default must be (expressly) 'due to materials or workmanship not in accordance with this Agreement'. No such qualification is stated in the other forms. Whilst, most of the time, a defect will necessarily arise out of materials or workmanship not in accordance with the contract, this will not always be the case. Consider, for example, hairline cracks arising in plasterwork some months after completion. This is often to be expected and is not a reflection of either bad materials or workmanship. Unless covered by the phrase 'excessive shrinkage', it is doubtful whether rectification of such cracks would be covered by the *Minor Works* standard form. However, under the main *Standard Form* it is likely to be covered either by 'shrinkages' (note: not *'excessive* shrinkages') or 'faults'.

2.3 PRACTICAL COMPLETION: WHEN DEFECTS LIABILITY COMMENCES

The key to commencement of the defects liability period under the JCT suite is **practical completion**. What this quite means has been subject to little judicial consideration, but the following cases shed some light on the meaning.

Westminster Corpn v Jarvis & Sons (1970)

The dispute involved a contract in the RIBA standard form (Local Authorities edition) (With Quantities). The contractor had agreed to construct a multi-storey car park for the employer, who had nominated a specific subcontractor to carry out the piling work ('the nominated subcontractor'). The nominated subcontractor purported to complete that work by the due date for its completion, and left site. Thereafter, many of the piles were discovered to be defective. Remedial works were carried out by the nominated subcontractor whereby progress of the main contract works was delayed. The question before the court was whether the contractor was entitled to an extension of time for completion of those works, because of the delay caused by the nominated subcontractor. In turn, this required their Lordships to consider the nature of practical completion in the context of a defects liability scheme.

Lord Justice Salmon in the Court of Appeal ([1969] 1 WLR 1448 at 1458), and Viscount Dilhorne in the House of Lords, came to starkly different views. It is helpful to understand both views.

- In the Court of Appeal, Salmon LJ considered that 'practical completion' meant completion for all practical purposes, that is to say, for the purpose of allowing the employers to take possession of the works and use them as intended. If completion in clause 21 meant completion down to the last detail, however trivial and unimportant, then clause 22 would be a penalty clause and as such unenforceable. Thus, it was suggested that practical completion could take place once the employer could take beneficial possession of the works, and (presumably) notwithstanding the existence of defects or outstanding works providing that these do no impact upon beneficial possession.

- By contrast, Viscount Dilhorne considered that what was meant was the completion of all the construction work that has to be done. This interpretation was supported in his Lordship's view by the fact that the defects liability period ran from the date in the practical completion certificate. After considering the defects liability provisions (which were in material terms identical to clause 17 of the 1998 JCT Standard Form), Viscount Dilhorne stated:

  'From these provisions there are, in my opinion, two conclusions to be drawn: first, that the issue of the certificate of practical completion determines the date of completion, which may, of course, be before or after the date specified for that in the contract, and, secondly, that the defects liability period is provided in order to enable defects not apparent at the date of practical completion to be remedied. If they had been then apparent, no such certificate would have been issued. It follows that a practical completion certificate can be issued when owing to latent defects, the works do not fulfil the contract requirements and that under the contract works can be completed despite the presence of such defects. Completion under the contract is not postponed until defects which became apparent only after the work had been finished have been remedied.'

P & M Kaye Ltd v Hosier & Dickinson Ltd (1972)

This case is considered in more detail in the context of 'temporary disconformity' (see Chapter 3). In the context of the definition of 'practical completion', however, Lord Diplock considered that the construction contract could be split into two defined periods:

- *The first period* continues until the contractor has completed the works (in the JCT Standard Form Contract, to the satisfaction of the architect) so far as the absence of any patent defects in materials or workmanship are concerned. This first period then ends with the issue by the architect of a certificate of practical completion under the equivalent of clause 17(1). This is the date of completion for the purpose of determining whether or not the contractor is in breach of his obligation to complete the works by the date so designated in the contract. The contractor then surrenders possession of the works to the employer, and the defects liability period starts. Importantly, Lord Diplock considered that where the employer takes possession of a part of the works before practical completion of the whole, the construction period for that part ends and the defects liability period for it begins.

  Thus, it appears that (notwithstanding that there may be no obligation upon the employer to do so) if the employer in fact takes beneficial possession of the site or part of it, it is to be deemed practically complete (at least for the purposes of liquidated damages).

- *The second period* is then the defects liability period. Its minimum duration is specified in the contract. If latent defects are discovered during this minimum period, it is extended until the contractor has made them good and the architect has so certified. During this second period the contractor's obligation is to make good to the satisfaction of the architect any latent defects that may become apparent.

H W Nevill (Sunblest) Ltd v William Press & Son Ltd (1981)

His Honour Judge Newey QC took a view which, whilst not incompatible with Viscount Dilhorne's approach, softened the definition of practical completion slightly. Judge Newey QC found that the word 'practically' in the equivalent of clause 17(1) of the 1998 JCT Standard Form gave the architect a discretion to certify that the contractor had fulfilled its obligations under the contract where de minimis (or very minor) work had not been carried out. However, in line with Viscount Dilhorne, he stated that if there were any patent defects in what the contractor had done the architect could not have given a certificate of practical completion.

2.3.1 Summary

From these cases, it is possible to discern the following guiding principles:

- As at the date of practical completion, the works should be complete. This means that the works should not include any patent defects.

- The works can be practically complete notwithstanding the presence of latent defects (as yet undiscovered).

- The employer's taking possession of the site is linked to the practical completion.

- The defects liability period is provided so that defects *which are not apparent at the date of practical completion* can be rectified.

- There is a discretion to certify practical completion where there exist minor or de minimis work to be carried out, but beyond that a certificate of practical completion should not be granted.

2.4 DEFECTS AND PRACTICAL COMPLETION: IN PRACTICE

It is a blurred line between what might be considered a 'patent defect' and what is to be considered de minimis and which does not have to hold up the certification of practical completion, subject to the discretion of the architect (under the JCT *Standard Form*) or the employer (under the JCT *Design and Build Standard Form*). These minor items are often referred to as 'snagging' items, and in practice are usually dealt with by the issuing of a list of such items to be rectified when practical completion is certified. There is, however, no specific mechanism under the JCT contracts for this to take place. It should therefore be noted that:

- the contractor is reliant upon the discretion of the architect or employer in this regard, who would be entitled to insist upon completion of all snagging items (which can really only be considered, upon analysis, as minor defects) prior to certifying practical completion;

- the architect or contract administrator would owe a duty of care to the employer not to certify practical completion when any item which should be considered as more than a de minimis defect remains. Such a professional would be well advised to:

  – exercise his discretion with care. By wrongfully issuing a certificate whilst patent defects exist, the architect would be potentially depriving the employer of his right to liquidated damages;

  – obtain a written undertaking from the contractor in relation to items remaining outstanding;

  – obtain the employer's consent to the issue of a practical completion certificate if in reality the snagging list arguably contains more significant items;

  – ensure that any retention would be sufficient to rectify the outstanding matters should the contractor not do so.

2.5 THE JCT MAJOR PROJECTS FORM: PRACTICAL COMPLETION DEFINED

The JCT *Major Projects Form* ('MPF') is of specific interest given that it seeks expressly to define practical completion. The definition is as follows:

'Practical Completion takes place when the Project is complete for all practical purposes and, in particular:

- The relevant statutory Requirements have been complied with and any necessary consents or approvals obtained;

- Neither the existence nor the execution of minor outstanding works would affect its use;

- Any stipulations identified by the Requirements as being essential for Practical Completion to take place have been satisfied, and

- The health and safety file and all "as built" information and operating and maintenance

> information required by the Contract to be delivered at Practical Completion has been so delivered to the Employer.'

The definition of 'Practical Completion' from the Major Projects Form, © the Joint Contracts Tribunal Limited 1998, publisher Sweet & Maxwell, is reproduced here with permission.

Thus, it seems that this definition is somewhat closer to Salmon LJ's definition in the Court of Appeal in *Jarvis*, in that outstanding matters which do not affect the use of the works do not of themselves (and providing they might be considered 'minor' in the context of the project) serve to prevent practical completion from having taken place.

2.6 ICE CONDITIONS OF CONTRACT (7TH EDITION)

By contrast to the JCT standard forms, which (save for the MPF) contain no specific mechanism by which practical completion may be certified notwithstanding outstanding works (although, pursuant to the decision in *H W Nevill v William Press* above, it would seem that there is such a discretion in relation to de minimis matters), the Institution of Civil Engineers (ICE) *Conditions of Contract* (7th edition) does make such provision through the concept of 'substantial completion'. See clauses 48 and 49:

'CERTIFICATE OF STANDARD COMPLETION

48(1) When the Contractor considers that:

the whole of the Works or

any Section in respect of which a separate time for completion is provided in the Appendix to the Form of Tender has been substantially completed and has satisfactorily passed any final test that may be prescribed by the Contract he may give notice in writing to that effect to the Engineer or to the Engineer's Representative. Such notice shall be accompanied by an undertaking to finish any outstanding work in accordance with the provisions of clause 49(1).

...

OUTSTANDING WORK AND DEFECTS

Work outstanding

49(1) The undertaking to be given under clause 48(1) may after agreement between the Engineer and the Contractor specify a time or times within which the outstanding work shall be completed. If no such times are specified any outstanding work shall be completed as soon as practicable during the Defects Correction Period.

Carry out of work of repair

49(2) The Contractor shall deliver up to the Employer the Works and each Section and part thereof at or as soon as practicable after the expiry of the relevant Defects Correction Period in the condition required by the Contract (fair wear and tear excepted) to the satisfaction of the Engineer. To this end the Contractor shall as soon as practicable carry out all work of repair, amendment, reconstruction, rectification and making good of defects of whatever nature as may be required of him in writing by the Engineer during the relevant Defects Correction Period or within 14 days after its expiry as a result of an inspection made by or on behalf of the Engineer prior to its expiry.

Cost of work of repair etc

49(3) All work required under Sub-clause (2) of this clause shall be carried out by the Contractor at his own expense if in the Engineer's opinion it is necessary due to the use of materials or workmanship not in accordance with the Contract or to neglect or failure by the Contractor to comply with any of his obligations under the Contract. In any other event the value of such work shall be ascertained and paid for as if it were additional work.

Remedy on Contractor's failure to carry out work required

49(4) If the Contractor fails to do any such work as aforesaid the Employer shall be entitled to carry out that work by his own workpeople or by other contractors and if it is work which the Contractor should have carried out at his own expense the Employer shall be entitled to recover the cost thereof from the Contractor and may deduct the same from any monies that are or may become due to the Contractor.'

Clauses from the ICE Conditions of Contract (7th edition) are reproduced with permission, Institution of Civil Engineers.

Up to the 7th edition, the ICE contract referred to 'maintenance' which (as set out below – see 2.8) can impose wider obligations than merely correction of defects. Clauses 48 and 49:

- provide a scheme whereby substantial completion can be issued notwithstanding the existence of some outstanding work;

- give the contractor both the right and the obligation to carry out rectification work in relation to defects;

- oblige the contractor to carry out repairs relating not just to his own work, but may also include defects arising, for example, from a design defect. In the latter case, the cost of carrying out the repair work does not fall to the contractor;

- give the employer the right to carry out repair work should the contractor fail to do so, and to deduct the costs from any monies to be paid to the contractor *if* the work carried out by the employer is work for which the contractor would have been liable to carry out *at his own expense*. Therefore, it seems that if the contractor fails to carry out rectification work arising, for example, out of a design defect and in relation to which he would have been entitled to additional payment, there is no sanction under the contract. Whilst technically the contractor would be in breach, it is difficult to see how any damages recoverable would be other than nominal.

2.7 PRACTICAL COMPLETION AND SUBSTANTIAL PERFORMANCE: THE SAME THING?

Big Island Contracting (HK) v Skink (1990)

The contract provided that 25 per cent of the price was payable upon practical completion, which was not otherwise defined. The contractor contended that practical completion had been achieved, and appealed the first instance decision that it had not been achieved on account of the existence of defects which would have cost between 10 per cent and 15 per cent of the contract price to rectify. It was held, dismissing the appeal, that practical completion could not be distinguished from 'substantial performance'. The court referred to Somervell LJ in *Hoenig v Issacs* (1952) which identified the question as:

'... whether in a contract for work and labour for a lump sum payable on completion the defendant can repudiate liability under the contract on the ground that the work though "finished" or "done" is in some respects not in accordance with the contract'.

The HK Court of Appeal held that as the work could not be considered 'finished' or 'done' in the light of the defects, practical completion had not been achieved.

It is doubtful that the concept of substantial performance is of much assistance in determining practical completion for the purposes of the JCT standard forms, but *Big Island* may well be useful in considering other contracts which link the concept of 'practical completion' to payment of some part or all of the contract price.

2.8 NEW ENGINEERING CONTRACTS STANDARD FORM (NEC 3RD EDITION)

The NEC *Engineering and Construction Contract* defines a 'defect' as follows:

'A Defect is:

- part of the works which is not in accordance with the Works Information;

- a part of the works designed by the Contractor which is not in accordance with the applicable law or the Contractor's design which the Project Manager has accepted.'

The NEC identifies the obligations of the contractor both during the contract period and also during the defects correction period.

'42. Searching for and notifying Defects

42.1 Until the defects date, the Supervisor may instruct the Contractor to search for a Defect. He gives his reason for the search with his instruction. Searching may include:

- Uncovering, dismantling, re-covering and re-erecting work;

- Providing facilities, materials and samples for tests and inspections done by the Supervisor;

- Doing tests and inspections which the Works Information does not require.

42.2 Until the defects date, the Supervisor notifies the Contractor of each Defect as soon as he finds it.

43. Correcting Defects

43.1 The Contractor corrects a Defect whether or not the Supervisor notifies him of it.

43.2 The Contractor corrects a notified Defect before the end of the defect correction period. The defect correction period begins at Completion for Defects notified before Completion and when the Defect is notified for other Defects.

43.3 The Supervisor issues the Defects Certificate at the later of the defects date and the end of the last defect correction period. The Employer's rights in respect of a Defect which the Supervisor has not found or notified are not affected by the issue of the Defects Certificates.

43.4 The Project Manager arranges for the Employer to allow the Contractor access to and use of a part of the works which he has taken over if they are needed for correcting a Defect. In this case the defect correction period begins when the necessary access and use have been provided.

44. Accepting Defects

44.1 The Contractor and the Project Manager may each propose to the other that the Works Information should be changed so that a Defect does not have to be corrected.

44.2 If the Contractor and the Project Manager are prepared to consider the change, the Contractor submits a quotation for reduced Prices or an earlier Completion Date or both to the Project Manager for acceptance. If the Project Manager accepts the quotation he gives an instruction to change the Works Information, the Prices and Completion Date accordingly.

45. Uncorrected Defects

45.1 If the Contractor is given access in order to correct a notified Defect but he has not corrected it within its defect correction period, the Project Manager assesses the cost to the Employer of having the Defect corrected by other people and the Contractor pays this amount. The Works Information is treated as having been changed to accept the Defect.

45.2 If the Contractor is not given access in order to correct a notified Defect before the defects date, the Project Manager assesses the cost to the Contractor of correcting the Defect and the Contractor pays this amount. The Works Information is treated as having been changed to accept the Defect.'

Clauses from the NEC3 Engineering and Construction Contract are reproduced here with permission from NEC Contracts.

The effect of these clauses under the NEC Form is as follows:

- Completion (as defined) can only take place when the contractor has corrected those notified defects which would have prevented the employer from using the works and others from doing their work.

- The defects correction period is to be agreed upon by the parties as a number of weeks. This runs from the date agreed as completion.

- In relation to defects notified during the defect correction period following completion, it appears that there remains the defined 'defect correction period' in which to correct the defect.

- The cost basis for deductions from the prices depends upon whether the contractor was granted access but did not carry out the rectification work (assessed as cost to employer) or was not granted access (assessed as cost to contractor).

- The right to remedy defects is not absolute, but dependent upon the granting of access. However, the deductible cost in relation to the defect will be lower if the contractor is not given the opportunity to remedy the defect.

2.9 DISTINCTION BETWEEN MAINTENANCE/DEFECTS PROVISIONS: OBLIGATION TO MAINTAIN WORKS IS WIDER THAN JUST TO MAKE GOOD DEFECTS

The nature and extent of the obligations upon a contractor will be defined by the terms of the contract. However, an obligation to maintain the works is likely to impose a wider duty than a requirement to repair defects.

Sevenoaks, Maidstone and Tunbridge Railway v London, Chatham and Dover Railway Company (1879)

A dispute arose involving consideration of the extent of a duty to 'make and maintain' a railway. The context of the dispute was, however, whether the duty *permitted* Chatham and Dover to build of a set of steps, which Sevenoaks objected to and sought the removal of. It was said there was no right to have built the steps, as part of a power to maintain. Whilst finding that it was 'very difficult to define what works of maintenance are', it was considered that it was a wide term, such that useful or reasonable ameliorations were not excluded by it. Thus, the maintenance obligation was stated to include any reasonable improvement. Maintenance may constitute keeping the subject in the same state, but may also consist of improving the state, bearing in mind that it must be maintenance as distinguished from alteration of purpose.

Brecknock and Abergavenny Canal Navigation v Pritchard (1796)

An obligation to repair may include rebuilding of parts destroyed by flood or fire. However, subject to express terms, this is likely to be subject to the principle of frustration if the works are substantially destroyed: see *Appleby v Myers* below.

Appleby v Myers (1867)

Appleby contracted to erect certain machinery on Myers' premises at specific prices for particular portions of work, and to keep it in repair for two years. The price was to be paid upon completion of the two-year period. After some sections of the work had been finished, and others were in the course of completion, the premises with all the machinery and materials were destroyed by an accidental fire. It was held that the contract was frustrated and the liability (on both sides) ceased.

2.9.1 Wear and tear

It is thought that a maintenance obligation would ordinarily extend to repair or replacement caused by wear and tear. Some standard forms define the requirements during the defects liability period so as specifically to exclude repairing normal wear and tear (see e.g. clause 37 of the IChemE 'Red Book' standard form).

2.10 DEFECTS LIABILITY: NOT AN EXCLUSIVE REMEDY

A question that has been raised on a number of occasions in the courts is the extent to which the defects liability provisions limit the employer's rights. In summary:

- The employer's entitlement to require the rectification of defects depends at least to some degree upon the contractor being notified in relation to the defects, and being granted access to remedy the same. Thus, while (for example) the NEC 3rd edition imposes an obligation upon the contractor to repair defects whether or not he is notified of them (clause 43.1), the basis upon which the contractor may be charged for the existence of an uncorrected defect expressly depends upon the granting of access to correct a notified defect (see 2.7 above).

- In general terms:
  - if the contractor is given notice of a defect but fails to correct it, then the employer may recover the cost to it of having the defect rectified by others;
  - if, however, no notice is given of a patent defect which arose during the relevant contractual period, or access is not granted to the contractor to allow remedial works, recovery by the employer will be

limited to the amount it would have cost the contractor to remedy the defect.

- The defects liability provisions are generally regarded as being *in addition to* the rights the employer would otherwise have simply by reason of the defect constituting a breach of contract.

- Therefore, the underlying rights of the employer by reason of the breach of contract which has given rise to the defect will not be affected by operation or non-operation of the defects liability provisions.

Hancock v Brazier (1966)

The defendants, builders and vendors of houses, were sued by the plaintiff purchaser following the emergence of cracking to the walls and floor of their property which resulted from the construction of foundations using unsuitable hardcore. The defendants sought to persuade the court that following completion, the purchaser's rights and remedies were limited by clause 11 of the contract, which provided that:

> 'If the purchaser shall discover any structural defects in the said house and works within six months from the date of completion and shall notify the vendor thereof in writing the vendor shall forthwith make good such structural defects without expense to the purchaser.'

In the Court of Appeal, Lord Denning MR emphasised that a builder will only be excused liability for defective work by clear words, and that clause 11 only applied to defects discovered within six months, not thereafter. Clause 11 only compelled the vendor to make good structural defects, but it did not excuse him from liability in damages. It is interesting to note that Lord Denning took a wider view than that of Diplock LJ at first instance, who held that clause 11 was of narrow application and would not, for example, operate so as to catch all defects emanating from breach of an obligation to carry out the works in a proper and workmanlike manner.

P & M Kaye Ltd v Hosier & Dickinson Ltd (1972)

Lord Diplock considered that a defects liability clause imposes upon the contractor a liability to mitigate the damage caused by his breach by making good the defects of construction at his own expense. It confers upon him a corresponding right to do so. It was thought to be a necessary implication from this that the employer cannot, as he otherwise could, recover as damages from the contractor the difference between the value of the works if they had been constructed in conformity with the contract and their value in their defective condition, without first giving to the contractor the opportunity of making good the defects.

The obverse of this is that the contractor is under an obligation to remedy the defects in accordance with the architect's instructions. If he does not do so, the employer can recover as damages the cost of remedying the defects, even though this cost is greater than the diminution in value of the works as a result of the unremedied defects.

(See also 3.2 in relation to this case.)

H W Nevill (Sunblest) Ltd v William Press & Sons Ltd (1981)

The defendants were contractors employed under a JCT Standard Form contract for the first phase of works to build a bakery. The second phase was to be carried out by other contractors. Defects were discovered in the drain systems installed by the defendants after the issue of the certificate of practical completion. The defendants returned to site and carried out remedial works identified by the architect, pursuant to the defect liability provisions.

The plaintiff brought proceedings for consequential losses in respect of delay, additional professional fees and loss of use of the building. The defendants argued that as the defects had been put right, they were not in breach and therefore not liable in damages.

HHJ Newey QC rejected the defendants' argument, stating that the defects liability provisions:

- were intended only to provide an efficient way of dealing with any defects which were discovered; and
- in the absence of clear words would not operate so as to limit the employer's remedy in damages.

Raymond Construction v Low Yang Tong and another (1988)

The plaintiffs were employed under a Singapore Institute of Architects standard form of contract to carry out building work on the first defendant's house and brought proceedings for outstanding payments. The defendant counterclaimed, amongst other things, for the cost of repairing defects (details of which were supplied to the plaintiffs) after the expiration of the defects liability period. The plaintiffs contended that by reason of the defects liability provisions, any claim against the plaintiff brought after the expiration of the defects liability period was not permitted.

Following *Hancock* and *H W Nevill*, Kan Ting Chiu J construed the defects liability provisions strictly, holding that it was only intended to deal efficiently with part of a situation caused by breaches of contract; upon its proper interpretation, the defendant's remedies were not limited to those set out in the defects liability provisions.

(See also 2.12 in relation to this case.)

William Tomkinson Ltd v The Parochial Church Council of St Michael (1990)

Where defects were not remedied by the contractor within the construction period, it was held that there was nothing in the wording of clause 2.5 of the JCT *Minor Works Contract* (see above) to suggest that it was intended to exclude the employer's ordinary right to damages for breach of contract, including the right to recover the cost of remedying defective workmanship.

HHJ Stannard referred to the dicta of Edmund Davies LJ in *Billyack v Leyland Construction Company Ltd* (1968) at 787 E–F, stating that:

'… it requires very clear words to debar a building owner from exercising his ordinary rights of suing if the work done is not in accordance with the contract'.

He also relied upon Lord Diplock in *Gilbert-Ash (Northern) Ltd v Modern Engineering (Bristol) Ltd* (1974) at 717H, who stated that:

'In construing such a contract, one starts with the presumption that neither party intends to abandon any remedies for its breach arising by operation of law, and clear express words must be used in order to rebut this presumption.'

HHJ Stannard considered that clause 2.5 was not such a provision.

Pearce and High v Baxter and Baxter (1999)

It was held that the giving of notice can be regarded as a condition precedent to the employer's right to require compliance with the clause (although different considerations might arise if the contractor became aware of the defects from some other source).

However, the Court of Appeal rejected the submission, based upon Lord Diplock's words in *P & M Kaye v Hosier & Dickinson* (above) that notice was a condition precedent to any claim arising out of defects appearing within the defects liability period. Instead, the contractor is liable for the defect, but is not liable for the full cost of repairs. It was held that the employer cannot recover more than the amount that it would have cost the contractor himself to remedy the defects. Thus, the employer's failure to comply with clause 2.5, whether by refusing to allow the contractor to carry out the repair or by failing to give notice of the defects, limits the amount of damages which he is entitled to recover.

As a matter of legal analysis, this result is achieved by permitting the contractor to set off against the employer's damages claim the amount by which he, the contractor, has been disadvantaged by not being able or permitted to carry out the repairs himself, or more simply, by reference to the employer's duty to mitigate his loss.

Whilst, therefore, the question of notification goes principally to the quantification of the employer's loss rather than the substantive right for damages for breach of contract by reason of the existence of a defect, there may be circumstances where, upon a proper construction of the contract, the giving of notice is a condition precedent to making a claim.

(See also 2.11 in relation to this case.)

London and SW Railway v Flower (1875)

The defendants were obliged under a private Act to maintain a bridge forming part of the plaintiff's railway, and to indemnify the plaintiff in respect of such maintenance costs. The plaintiffs carried out remedial works to the bridge without affording the defendants the opportunity to effect the repairs. Brett J held that on a proper construction of the Act, the absence of a notice of disrepair was fatal to the plaintiff's claim for recover their outlay. As the railway was in the exclusive possession of the plaintiff, the defendants would not be aware of the existence of any defects which they were obliged to repair unless express notice of such defects was provided.

Whether or not a notice is required, and the precise effect of its absence, will of course depend upon a proper construction of the relevant contractual provision.

2.11 WHAT DEFECTS ARE CAUGHT BY A DEFECTS LIABILITY PROVISION?

Whilst it is of course dependent upon the wording of the clause, it is usually only defects that *appear* during the defects liability period which are caught by its provisions, both in terms of giving the contractor the *obligation* to make good, but also the *right* to make good. The proper operation of the defects liability clause will therefore depend to an extent upon the proper certification of practical, or substantial, completion (as the case may be). If a defect pre-exists the certificate, the certificate should not have been issued. However, such a pre-existing defect cannot then be said to 'appear' during the defects liability period. It is for this reason that it is important that an architect or contract administrator is careful to ensure that the contractor acknowledges his obligation to rectify any minor patent defects which the architect or contract administrator has decided (in the exercise of his discretion), should not hold up the issue of the certificate. See generally the cases on practical completion, above.

Subject potentially to any difficulties caused by improper administration of the contract, the defects liability clause will be construed strictly and will not apply to defects other than those that fall within its express terms.

Marsden Urban District Council v Sharp (1931)

The defendant contractors were engaged by the plaintiff council to construct a road over moorland. The contract contained the following term:

'Should it at any time subsequent to the termination of the period of maintenance up to but not exceeding a period of five years from the date of the completion of the works be discovered that the terms of this specification have been violated by the execution of bad, insufficient or inaccurate work the council shall be at liberty to make good such work and to recover the cost thereof from the contractor.'

The council discovered defects in the concrete used to construct the road. Such discoveries were made in different areas both prior to and after the expiration of the maintenance period. The council sought to argue that as a violation of the specification as to concrete had been discovered, the cost of replacing all of the concrete was recoverable under the above clause, irrespective of the actual area of defective concrete discovered during the maintenance period. The judge, however, held that the clause only covered defects appearing within five years and to the extent of that appearance. Consequently, damages were only recoverable in respect of the defects which manifested themselves prior to the expiration of the maintenance period.

Pearce and High v Baxter and Baxter (1999)

It was held by the Court of Appeal that the phrase 'defects [etc.] which appear' during the period should be read objectively, as a description of those defects to which the clause applies. The defect must therefore become apparent, meaning become patent rather than remain latent, during the notice period, regardless of whether any particular person has actual knowledge of it.

(See also 2.10 in relation to this case.)

2.12 EFFECT OF FINAL CERTIFICATE

The JCT Standard Form has clauses which provide that the final certificate has a conclusive effect, subject to dispute resolution provisions. These clauses (and similar clauses) are obviously of great importance when considering what liabilities a contractor may have in relation to defects following the completion of the works.

Crown Estates Commissioners v John Mowlem & Co Ltd (1994)

The dispute related to the effect of clause 30.9.1 of the JCT *Standard Form of Contract, Private With Quantities*, 1980 edition. This clause stated:

> 'Except as provided in clauses 30.9.2 and 30.9.3 (and save in respect of fraud) the Final Certificate shall have effect in any proceedings arising out of or in connection with this Contract (whether by arbitration under article 5 or otherwise) as conclusive evidence that where the quality of materials or the standard of workmanship are to be to the reasonable satisfaction of the Architect the same are to such satisfaction ...'

It was held that the certificate applies its conclusive effect as regards quality of materials and standard of workmanship to all materials and workmanship where approval of such matters was inherently something for the opinion of the architect. This conclusion was of broad import, and clearly had a restrictive effect upon the ability to bring a claim for defects after the issue of the final certificate.

- Since the decision in *Crown Estates* it should be noted that JCT have amended the terms of clause 30.9.1 in the 1998 edition of the Standard Form (and its equivalent in the 2005 suite).

- The conclusive effect is limited to those matters in relation to which it was expressly stated in the contract documents would be to the reasonable satisfaction of the architect.

- It remains the case that the binding effect of the final certificate is capable of substantively affecting the rights of the employer in relation to certain defects.

London Borough of Hackney & Dagenham v Terrapin Construction (2000)

This case considered the conclusive effect of a final statement under the JCT *With Contractor's Design Standard Form* 1981 edition. It was held that there is no logical distinction between statutory requirements on the one hand and contractual obligations on the other. The agreement provided that the final account and final statement were conclusive evidence as to the quality of materials and the standards of workmanship, and this also extended to any relevant statutory requirements. It was also considered that the JCT *With Contractor's Design* distinguished between design on the one hand and construction or workmanship (i.e. 'works' and 'materials') on the other. The 'conclusive evidence' defence was held only to be available in relation to workmanship, although this conclusion was in part derived from the terms of the design warranty on the part of contractor in that particular agreement.

(It is thought that the same reasoning would apply to the most recent JCT *Design and Build Contract* 2005. This would obviously mean that defects arising out of design are capable of being treated differently to other defects.)

Billyack v Leyland Construction Company Ltd (1968)

In this case, the defendants undertook to build and complete a dwelling house 'in a workmanlike manner' and in accordance with a specification annexed to the contract. The specification obliged the defendants to carry out works in accordance with local authority byelaws and to the satisfaction of the local authority. Further, the release of the second payment under the contract was contingent upon the issue of a 'certificate of habitation' by the local authority which was to stand as 'conclusive evidence of the completion of the dwelling house'.

Following the issue of the certificate of habitation, the plaintiffs discovered numerous structural defects to the property and issued proceedings. The judge held that whilst the certificate was conclusive evidence of the times fixed for payments under the agreement, it was not conclusive evidence that the house had been completed in a workmanlike manner. Following *Hancock v Brazier*, Edmund Davies LJ emphasised that very clear words were required to debar a building owner from exercising his ordinary rights of suing if the work done is not in accordance with the contract.

NCB v William Neill (1985)

The parties entered into a written contract in respect of construction works at the plaintiff's colliery. The contract contained a clause stipulating that works carried out by the defendant building contractors were to be executed in the manner set out in the specifications and to the reasonable satisfaction of the project engineer. Upon completion of the works, a certificate of satisfaction was issued to the defendant by the project engineer. Subsequently, some of the structures erected as part of the contract works collapsed. The defendant sought to argue that the certificate of satisfaction was conclusive of the completion of the works in accordance with the contract, effectively barring the plaintiff's claim. The judge rejected the defendant's contentions, holding that the clause imposed two obligations, viz: (i) to complete the works to the satisfaction of the project engineer; and (ii) to complete the works according to the specifications. The fact that a certificate had been issued did not absolve the defendant from its obligations to complete the works in accordance with the standards required by the contract.

Raymond Construction v Low Yang Tong and another (1988)

(The facts of this case are set out at 2.10 above.) Whilst the judge rejected the argument that the defects liability clauses limited the defendant's exposure to a claim arising out of defects, he did suggest that the issue of a final certificate that the works had been properly carried out and completed in accordance with the terms of the contract would have 'lent support' to the plaintiff's cause.

3
'Temporary disconformity'

3.1 INTRODUCTION

Since Lord Diplock's dissenting speech in *P & M Kaye v Hosier & Dickinson* (see 3.2 below), there has been a theory that a contractor who carries out defective work during the course of the contract is not in breach of contract until completion and handover, because it is open to him to rectify his work. This chapter reviews the origin of the theory, its treatment in subsequent judgments and its likely present status.

3.2 THE CASES

P & M Kaye Ltd v Hosier & Dickinson Ltd (1972)

(See also 2.10 above in relation to this case.) Pursuant to a JCT Standard Form contract, the claimant contractors agreed to build a warehouse and offices for the defendant employers. The contractors took out a summons under RSC, Ord 14, for judgment in the sum of £14,861, based on the architect's interim certificates which remained unpaid. The employers alleged defective work and that they had suffered damage, namely, £13,464 loss of profits, thereby; they were given leave to defend on payment of £5,000. The parties agreed that the action would be left in abeyance until such rectification works as may have been required were carried out. Two years later the architect issued his final certificate for an outstanding balance of £2,360. Issues arose between the parties as to the conclusive effect of the final certificate, in the light of the existence of the first litigation. The theory of temporary disconformity arose out of the dissenting judgment of Lord Diplock, when he stated as follows:

'During the construction period it may, and generally will, occur that from time to time some part of the works done by the contractor does not initially conform with the terms of the contract either because it is not in accordance with the contract drawings or the contract bills or because the quality of the workmanship or materials is below the standard required by condition 6(1). The contract places upon the contractor the obligation to comply with any instructions of the architect to remedy any temporary disconformity with the requirements of the contract. If it is remedied no loss is sustained by the employer unless the time taken to remedy it results in practical completion being delayed beyond the date of completion designated in the contract. In this event the only loss caused is that the employer is kept out of the use of his building beyond the date on which it was agreed that it should be ready for use. For such delay liquidated damages at an agreed rate are payable under condition 22 of the contract.

Upon a legalistic analysis it might be argued that temporary disconformity of any part of the works with the requirements of the contract even though remedied before the end of the agreed construction period constituted a breach of contract for which nominal damages would be recoverable. I do not think that makes business sense. Provided that the contractor puts it right timeously I do not think that the parties intended that any temporary disconformity should of itself amount to a breach of contract by the contractor.'

Lintest Builders v Roberts (1980)

Lintest was engaged by Mr Roberts to carry out conversion works to a dwelling-house. During the course of the project, Mr Roberts ran out of money and Lintest terminated the contract. It transpired that the works carried out had not been properly done and had not been remedied at the time of determination. The court held that but for the determination of the contract, the employer would have had the right to require the contractor to correct or remedy the bad work. That right arises at the time that work is done. It is a right which, when it arises, can be enforced under the provisions of the contract by suitable notices from the architect. Alternatively, if all goes well, it can be left over until the period when a certificate of practical completion is given.

Lord Justice Roskill doubted whether Lord Diplock had intended his comments to be of universal application.

- It would seem to follow that, at least where the employer has (through the architect or otherwise) an express right to give instructions relating to defective work, the temporary disconformity theory may be of limited application.

- It should be noted that the Court of Appeal specifically rejected the argument that if the employer's right had not been exercised, i.e. by giving an instruction to rectify the defective work, the correct analysis was that no rights had accrued.

- On the basis of *Lintest*, in a contract such as the NEC where the contractor is under a specific obligation throughout the contract to correct defects whether notified to him or not (3rd edition, clause 43.1), it is difficult to see any room to apply the theory of disconformity.

Nene Housing Society Ltd v The National Westminster Bank Ltd (1980)

The claimants sustained losses remedying a contractor's defective work and brought proceedings against the defendants under a performance bond that provided that liability should arise 'on default by the contractor'. The defendants sought to rely on Lord Diplock's judgment in *P & M Kaye v Hosier & Dickinson* (above) as authority for the proposition that defective work does not constitute a breach of contract. The submission was rejected: in *P & M Kaye v Hosier & Dickinson* the defects had been put right; on the present facts this was not the case.

Mocatta J also pointed out that the duty to complete the works was a dual obligation: i.e. both to *carry out* and to *complete* the works. Consequently, whilst the defect may be remedied before it affects the *completion* of the works, it will nevertheless constitute a breach of the obligation to *carry out* the works in accordance with the contract.

Where the contractor's obligations are expressed to be twofold in this manner, one can see how the theory of temporary disconformity might sensibly be rejected.

Conversely, if the obligation upon the contractor in a specific contract is simply 'to complete' the works, the scope for arguing that defective work during the carrying out of the project does not amount to a breach is enlarged.

William Tomkinson v Parochial Church Council of St Michael (1990)

This case concerned the operation of a defects liability provision in a standard form construction contract (specifically, clause 2.5 JCT 1980 edition).

William Tomkinson were employed by the defendants as contractors to carry out restoration works at a parish church in Liverpool. Some of the works were defective. Consequently, the architect arranged for other contractors to remedy such defects before certifying practical completion on 13 June 1985.

William Tomkinson brought an action for payment of sums certified in interim certificates. The defendants brought a counterclaim for defective workmanship.

The contractors, relying on Lord Diplock's judgment in *P & M Kaye v Hosier & Dickinson*, contended that they had the whole of the construction period in which to complete the works and that none of the works could be considered defective until that period had expired. They further argued that the defects liability provision conferred a right to remedy any defects in the three month period following practical completion, a right which had been denied by the engagement of alternative contractors.

HHJ Stannard held that where works fell short of the standard required by the contract, they properly constitute breaches, and the fact that the employer put them right will not absolve the contractor of liability. However, this was a case where instructions had been given in relation to the correction of defective work, which had remained unremedied. In these circumstances, it is easy to see how the contractor would not be able to rely upon a theory of temporary disconformity.

Surrey Heath Borough Council v Lovell Construction and Haden Young Ltd (1988)

Lovell, a firm of contractors, was engaged by the plaintiffs to design and construct an office building. Prior to practical completion, part of the building was damaged by fire. Although appropriate repairs were carried out by Lovell, the plaintiff brought a claim for consequential losses under clause 20.2 of the contract which obliged Lovell to indemnify the employer against any loss or damage contingent upon an omission, default or the negligence of Lovell or its subcontractors. HHJ Fox-Andrews QC held that 'temporary disconformity' was an unhelpful expression in circumstances where a building had been partially destroyed by fire. Even though Lovell had effected repairs to put right the damage, it was still in breach of contract and the plaintiff was entitled to recover its consequential losses. This conclusion related to consequential loss, but not to costs incurred by the employer in remedying defective work.

Guinness plc v CMD Property Developments Ltd (1995)

This case concerned defects arising out of refurbishment and extension works to a property in West London. The contractor submitted that a claim in damages was premature in circumstances where it had not been notified of the defects and given the opportunity to remedy the same. The court held that if there were any uncorrected defects then the contractor was under a liability to repair them. Put another way, a right had accrued to CMD to insist upon any outstanding defects to be corrected by the contractor, which was not extinguished by the absence of formal architect's notices. Such a right had a monetary value which was to be calculated by reference to the cost which the contractor would have incurred in correcting the defects.

Rice v Great Yarmouth Borough Council (2000)

In a claim concerning an alleged repudiatory breach of a maintenance contract, Lady Justice Hale in the Court of Appeal noted the parallels with building contracts, 'in the number and variety of the obligations involved and the varying gravity of the breaches which may be committed, some of which may be remediable and some not'. The court below had been correct to ask itself whether the cumulative breaches would continue to deliver a substandard performance. Thus, the concept of a contractor's work containing a sufficient extent of defects to warrant the grant of an immediate remedy – rather than waiting to the date for completion – was established as relevant.

This of itself is, again, somewhat contradictory to the temporary disconformity theory.

Foster Wheeler Wood Group Engineering Ltd v Chevron UK Ltd (1996)

Foster Wheeler's arguments were that its contract had been carefully drawn up so that the parties had set out a comprehensive code for what was to happen should a flaw be discovered in Foster Wheeler's work so that such a flow would not give rise to a breach of the agreement. His Honour Judge Humphrey Lloyd QC did not deal expressly with the 'vexed question' of whether the principle of temporary disconformity applied, but considered in any event that the question of whether there had been a breach may be a question of fact and degree.

Sutcliffe v Chippendale & Edmundson (1971)

Whilst no direct consideration of the theory of temporary disconformity was given (for obvious reasons: it had yet to be voiced), HHJ William Stabb considered that it was relevant to justifying an owner's termination of a contractor's employment that,

> '... the quality of work was deteriorating and the number of defects was multiplying, many of which [the architect] had tried unsuccessfully to have put right ... the contractors had neither the ability, competence or the will by this time to complete the work in the manner required by the contract'.

The extent of 'temporary disconformity' was such that not only was it to be regarded as a breach of contract, but that it was a repudiatory breach of contract.

Shawton Engineering Ltd v DGP International Ltd (2006)

The action concerned the provision of design drawings by the defendant for the engineering and manufacture of box encapsulation plant for the storage of nuclear waste. So far as the quality of DGP's drawings was concerned, the court was satisfied that many of the drawings contained errors, including a number of errors which a reasonably competent engineer would not have put forward. However, on the basis that the errors were in general corrected by DGP, the court considered that the existence of errors went essentially to the question of delay rather than breach of contract of itself. Whilst not expressed in terms of 'temporary disconformity', the judge's analysis was essentially one consistent with Lord Diplock's formulation.

Adkin v Brown (NZ) (2002)

In this New Zealand case, it was held that an employer was not permitted to terminate for breach of an essential stipulation as to structural safety, as the defects in question could have been remedied and completed for a relatively small sum. The New Zealand Court of Appeal, recognising that its decision was consistent with the so-called temporary disconformity theory, stated:

'It does not seem to us that the High Court Judge was denying the possibility that it might have been an essential breach to leave the building in an unsafe condition at the end of construction. The fact that the building's defects in that regard could be remedied and that it could be completed for such a relatively small sum (even by values of 1981) rather speaks for itself. It may be that in another case it could be shown that a failure to meet such a structural safety requirement during construction could give rise to a right of cancellation on the part of the owner. It was held not to be so in this case and, we think, understandably so.'

Eu Asia Engineering v Wing Hong Contractors (1990)

The Hong Kong High Court applied 'temporary disconformity' principles in relation to defective concreting works (specifically 'honeycombing'). Finding that honeycombing was a frequent occurrence in the construction industry which would have been made good in the normal course of work, Kaplan J dismissed the submission that it could give rise to termination. In relation to other defects (bulging and the concrete joints), Kaplan J expressly stated that these defects fell within Lord Diplock's observations.

3.3 SUMMARY

In analysing the issue of temporary disconformity, it is important not to lose sight of the circumstances in which reliance upon such a theory might be relevant.

- If *in fact* defects during the course of the works are rectified prior to completion, the only effect is likely to have been one of delay. This will usually be compensated by liquidated damages in a building contract, or otherwise by general damages caused by the prolongation of the contract period. It is unlikely, in these circumstances, that there would be anything other than nominal damages caused by the 'breach' (if it is such) during the course of the works.

- The question will be highly relevant if the employer terminates early, either pursuant to contractual termination provisions or by accepting the contractor's repudiatory breach. Indeed, the employer may wish to use defective work yet to be corrected in order to justify termination. As to this:

    - where there is an express right to instruct the contractor to remedy defective work, this should be exercised by the prudent employer;

    - in any event, an employer should be cautious in alleging that the contractor is in repudiatory breach of contract by reason of defective work which is obviously capable of remedy;

    - in more extreme circumstances (such as those in *Sutcliffe*) it is likely that temporary disconformity can give rise to not only breach, but repudiatory breach. A contractor guilty of such flagrant inadequacy is extremely unlikely to be able to pray Lord Diplock's words in aid;

    - however, as illustrated by *Adkin* and *Eu Asia*, an employer who relies upon the existence of defects that are, in the ordinary course of events, to be of the nature and degree that one might expect in a construction contract, may not succeed in establishing breach at all, far less repudiatory breach.

4
Claims for defective work in tort

4.1 INTRODUCTION

Assume that a homeowner enters into a contract with a builder for the design and construction of an extension to his property. The extension is duly completed, but it subsequently transpires that the design is defective, and cracking occurs. To remedy the fault, the extension will have to be demolished and rebuilt.

The above scenario is not unusual, and the homeowner's simplest recourse is to sue the builder for breach of contract in order to recover damages. As has been explored in Chapter 2, when two parties contract, the existence of a defect will ordinarily give rise to a cause of action for breach, and the contract may also have, in addition, defect liability provisions to be followed in the event that defects arise within a defined period.

However, the position is more complicated when there is no contractual relationship between the parties. Assume that the subsequent purchaser of the property described above attempts to sue the original builder when the cracking first appears, after purchasing the property. There may be a term in the original contract which confers third party rights onto the subsequent purchaser, in which case he may be able to bring proceedings as if he were the original homeowner (provided, of course, that the same are issued within the limitation period, as to which see Chapter 7). It might also be possible to bring a claim pursuant to the *Defective Premises Act* 1972, depending upon whether the defects render the property unfit for habitation (as to which, see Chapter 5).

However, absent any such statutory or contractual route to recovery, the subsequent purchaser will be forced to sue in tort.

And it is here that problems arise. The damage complained of by the subsequent purchaser is what is known as 'pure economic loss'. In simple terms, the purchaser has paid too much for his property as the defects only manifested themselves after purchase. Had he known of the defects prior to the sale, he would, in all likelihood, have offered less money or decided not to buy the property.

Unless the subsequent purchaser is able to prove that a 'special relationship', or heightened duty of care, exists between him and the original builder then recovery becomes decidedly more difficult, if not impossible. This chapter deals with claimants who have found themselves in similar situations.

4.2   REQUIREMENT FOR POSSESSORY TITLE

The minimum requirement for a would-be claimant is a possessory title in the damaged property; mere contractual rights over the same will not suffice.

Candlewood Navigation Corp v Mitsui Osk Lines (1986)

The plaintiff chartered a vessel which was involved in a collision with a negligently-piloted ship owned by the defendant. Following the collision, repairs to the chartered vessel were required and were carried out in Japan. Before the Supreme Court of New South Wales, the claimant successfully recovered damages in respect of the hire charges paid to the owner of the damaged vessel whilst repairs were being effected and for loss of profits during the same period. The Privy Council allowed the defendant's appeal, holding that as the claimant was a time charterer and not an owner of the vessel, it was not entitled to recover hire charges and loss of profits from the defendant whilst the vessel was not operational. A proprietary or possessory right in respect of a damaged chattel is required in order to bring an action against the tortfeasor for such damage.

4.3   DEFINITION OF 'DAMAGE'

Forster v Outred & Co (1982)

In legal terms, 'damage' is defined as any detriment, liability or loss capable of assessment in money terms.

D&F Estates Ltd v Church Commissioners for England (1989)

The third defendant was a contractor responsible for the construction of the block of flats built on land owned by the first defendant. Plastering work was carried out by subcontractors to the third defendant. Upon completion, the first defendant granted a lease of one of the flats to the plaintiffs, who then occupied the premises.

Some of the plasterwork was discovered to be defective in that it became loose and fell down onto the floors. The plaintiffs sued the defendant in negligence, claiming (amongst other things) the cost of appropriate remedial works, loss of rent whilst such works were carried out and the cost of cleaning carpets and other possessions which had been soiled by the falling plaster.

The House of Lords decided that in order to recover successfully in tort, any damage must be damage to property other than the property which is the product of the negligence (i.e. a claimant cannot recover for damage to a building caused by that building itself). This, it was considered, was 'pure economic loss' and therefore irrecoverable.

Murphy v Brentwood DC (1991)

Damage to a house that is attributable to a defect in the structure of the house is not recoverable in tort. The defect represents pure economic loss, which is only recoverable in contract or in tort by reason of some special relationship of proximity which imposes on the tortfeasor a duty of care to protect against economic loss.

Nitrigin Eireann Teoranta v Inco Alloys Ltd (1992)

The defendants were pipe manufacturers who supplied steel alloy tubing for use in the furnaces within the claimant's chemical factory. The tubing was installed in 1981. Cracking was discovered in a section of tubing (and repaired) in 1983. In 1984, the cracking occurred again, causing the tubing to burst and methane to leak into the surrounding furnace, triggering an explosion, damaging the same furnace and forcing the factory to shut down.

The claimant brought proceedings in negligence to recover damages for the cost of repairs to the plant, the cost of replacing the burst pipe and for loss of profits as a result of the shutdown of the factory.

The judge held that the cracking in 1983 was damage arising out of a defect in quality, but that as such damage was damage to the pipe itself, it was properly categorised as pure economic loss and thus irrecoverable in negligence.

However, the judge held that the claimants had a cause of action in negligence arising out of the second incidence of cracking in 1984, as the damage complained of (i.e. the damage to the furnace and the factory) constituted damage to 'other' property and was recoverable.

Pirelli General Cable Works Ltd v Oscar Faber & Partners (1983)

Consulting engineers were negligent in approving a design which contained an unsuitable lining for an industrial chimney. The chimney subsequently suffered cracking. The claim against the engineers in contract was time-barred, so the plaintiff brought proceedings in tort. It was held that the plaintiff's cause of action in tort arose when the physical damage to the chimney actually occurred, not when the defect causing such damage (in this case the use of unsuitable lining) occurred or was discovered.

(See also 7.4.1 in relation to this case.)

4.3.1 Summary

On the basis of these cases:

- it is important that the distinction between 'damage' and a 'defect' is clear;
- in simple terms, the defect is the 'flaw' in design, or workmanship; the defect may or may not give rise to damage;
- if there is any damage, the nature of the damage will:
  - dictate whether the person responsible for the flaw owed any duty of care to prevent that type of damage;
  - determine what (if any) loss is recoverable.

Using the example set out in the introduction to this chapter, the subsequent purchaser of the property may become aware of a defect in the design of the foundations to the extension, but:

- the 'damage' may consist of nothing more than superficial cracking to the plaster. The defect in one part of the extension has not therefore caused damage other than to another part of the extension;
- if this is the case, the 'damage' caused by the defect is likely to be restricted to:
  - the cost of carrying out repairs to the extension;
  - alternatively (or additionally) a loss in the value of the property;
- both of these are regarded by the law as 'pure economic loss';
- it is only possible in very limited circumstances to make recovery in tort for pure economic loss.

4.4 'SPECIAL RELATIONSHIP'

Where advice, statements or information is supplied to a known recipient for a particular purpose, a 'special relationship' grounding liability for 'pure economic loss' may be established. The supplier of the information will usually be aware of the purpose for which such information is sought, and liability will ensue in circumstances where it was justified for the recipient to rely upon the same.

Hedley Byrne & Co Ltd v Heller & Partners Ltd (1964)

The claimant advertising agents approached the defendants for a credit reference of a potential client prior to contracting on behalf of that client on terms which would have rendered the claimants personally liable should the client default. The credit reference was given free of charge and was favourable to the client. The claimants relied on the reference, which turned out to be misleading, and suffered loss. On the facts the defendants escaped liability on the basis that the credit reference was expressly provided 'without responsibility'; nevertheless, the case established the principle that a party may be liable for 'pure economic loss' in tort, as elucidated by Lord Morris (at 502–503):

'... it should now be regarded as settled that if someone possessed of a special skill undertakes, quite irrespective of contract, to apply that skill for the assistance of another person who relies upon such skill, a duty of care will arise ... Furthermore, if in a sphere in which a person is so placed that others could reasonably rely upon his judgment or his skill or upon his ability to make careful inquiry, a person takes it upon himself to give information or advice to, or allows his information or advice to be passed on to, another person who, as he knows or should know, will place reliance upon it, then a duty of care will arise'.

4.4.1 The application to the construction professionals and contractors

Henderson v Merrett Syndicates Ltd (1995)

The House of Lords stated (in a case unrelated to defects in a building) that because construction professionals, such as architects, may be responsible in tort for physical damage, it was difficult to see why in principle concurrent remedies in tort and contract should not also be available against members of other professions, whatever form the relevant damage may take.

However, it was also considered that the normal relationship between employer/building owner and subcontractor will not usually warrant the imposition of a heightened duty of care:

'... in many cases in which a contractual chain ... is constructed it may well prove to be inconsistent with an assumption of responsibility which has the effect of short-cutting the contractual structure so put in place by the parties ... [under] the ordinary building contract, the main contractor sub-contracts with sub-contractors or suppliers (often nominated by the building owner) ... [and] it will not ordinarily be open to the building owner to sue the sub-contractor or supplier direct under the *Hedley Byrne* principle'.

Storey v Charles Church Developments Ltd (1996)

The defendant was a building contractor who constructed a house for the claimant pursuant to a design and build contract. Following completion of the building works, structural cracking appeared which was attributable to defective foundation design. A claim in contract was statute-barred, so proceedings were brought in tort. HHJ Hicks QC concluded that a designer's concurrent duty in tort to use due care and skill extends to taking care not to cause economic loss unless the contractual duty is more limited.

Payne v Setchell (2002)

(The facts of this case are set out at 4.5 below.) The claimant's case was that he had, in purchasing a property, relied upon the defendants' certificate in respect of the original foundation works carried out for the original homeowner.

The court considered that *Murphy v Brentwood* (see 4.3 above) was a binding authority for the proposition that any person offering construction services is only ordinarily liable for physical injury or property damage but not for economic loss. However, on the facts the court found that the defendants were aware that their certificate was a document which was commonly used to satisfy a prospective purchaser as to the adequacy of foundations and, in the circumstances, the claimant had so relied upon it.

Tesco Stores Ltd v Costain Construction Ltd (2003)

Following a fire at the claimant's supermarket in Worcestershire, proceedings were brought against the defendant designers of the store, the claimant alleging that the spread of the fire was due to the absence of proper fire-stopping measures.

On the facts, the court found that the tortious duty owed by the defendant did encompass the avoidance of causing pure economic loss, viewing it as a natural consequence of entering into a contract with the claimant. The judge went on to comment on the judgment in *Payne v Setchell*:

> '… it does not seem to me that *Murphy v Brentwood District Council* and the other authorities … do establish the proposition that a builder **never** owes a duty of care which extends to not causing economic loss, only that he does not do so in the absence of *"a special relationship"*'.

Mirant Asia-Pacific Construction (HK) Ltd v Ove Arup & Partners (2005)

The defendant consulting engineers sought to rely on *Payne v Setchell* in arguing that, in the absence of a specific contractual term, a designer is not liable for economic loss. This argument was rejected and was not challenged on appeal. The court at first instance had held that if designers perform services of a professional/quasi-professional nature, they placed themselves in the same position as bankers and/or accountants, and owe a duty of care not to cause economic loss.

Mutual Life and Citizen's Assurance Co v Evatt (1971)

Payment for services is not a prerequisite for the existence of a 'special relationship'. In this case, the Privy Council held that gratuitous advice could attract liability in negligence if an informant gives such advice in the course of his profession and the informee suffers loss as a result.

Junior Books Ltd v Veitchi Co (1983)

The defendants were flooring subcontractors who were engaged to lay a floor at the pursuer's factory. The pursuer brought a claim in negligence against the defendants, alleging that the floor was laid defectively. During the course of laying the floor no physical damage was caused either to the materials themselves or to other property. The House of Lords held that a duty of care to prevent against economic loss consequential upon defective work would be upheld in the circumstances. It appears that this was justified on the basis that the defendants were nominated for their special skill and the employer was entitled to place direct reliance on them as a result.

[*Junior Books* is now usually considered to be at best confined to its own facts. Indeed, in *D&F Estates*, the House of Lords described it as 'unique'. It was, for example, recently distinguished in the case of *Architype Projects Ltd v Dewhurst Macfarlane & Partners* (2003). However, although it should be treated with extreme caution, it is worth noting that *Junior Books* was not expressly overruled in *Murphy v Brentwood*.]

Shanklin Pier Ltd v Detel Products Ltd (1951)

The claimant was the owner of a pier who engaged a contractor to carry out refurbishment works to the same. One of the contractor's tasks was to repaint the pier and, to this end, the defendant paint suppliers warranted to the claimant that its paint would adequately protect the pier against rust damage for seven to ten years. Acting upon such statements, the claimant instructed the contractor to procure paint supplies from the defendant. The paint failed to protect the pier, and the court held that damages were recoverable from the defendant even though the claimant was not a party to the contract for the supply of the paint.

4.4.2 Summary

- A construction professional might readily be subjected to a concurrent duty of care to prevent economic loss, by (for example) defective design, inspection or survey. The *concurrent* nature of the duty readily assumes a contractual relationship between the relevant parties.

- In the absence of a contractual relationship, some other 'special relationship' would be required, whether it is sought to impose the duty on a professional or a contractor. Usually, however, the manner in which the parties had decided to arrange their contractual relationships will be determinative of whether or not there is a 'special relationship' for the purpose of imposing tortious duties for defective work. Thus:

  - a nominated subcontractor will not ordinarily owe the employer or building owner a duty to guard against pure economic loss;

  - in principle at least, the existence of a 'special relationship' might on the facts be upheld if the services provided by the nominated subcontractor are particularly skilled and/or specialist;

  - a subcontractor may find itself liable for representations made in respect of defective services if they induce an employer to instruct the main contractor to produce such services.

4.5 THE 'COMPLEX STRUCTURE THEORY'

The 'complex structure theory' is based upon the proposition that a defect in one part of a property which manifests itself in a defect in another part of the property could be analysed as causing physical damage, rather than pure economic loss and thus avoiding the restrictions on recovery for pure economic loss in tort.

D&F Estates Ltd v Church Commissioners for England (1989)

(The facts of this case are set out at 4.3 above.) Lord Bridge and Lord Oliver concurred that there may be circumstances involving 'complex structures' or 'complex chattels', where certain elements of the structure in question could be regarded as being distinct from other elements; consequently, damage to one part of the structure caused by a hidden defect in another part may indeed qualify as damage to 'other property' ([1989] AC 177 at 207, per Lord Bridge):

> 'However, I can see that it may well be arguable that in the case of complex structures, as indeed possibly in the case of complex chattels, one element of the structure should be regarded for the purpose of the application of the principles under discussion as distinct from another element, so that damage to one part of the structure caused by a hidden defect in another part may qualify to be treated as damage to "other property", and whether the argument should prevail may depend on the circumstances of the case.'

It was further suggested that where remedial works were necessary to prevent imminent danger to people or (possibly) other property, then the costs of carrying out the same were potentially recoverable.

Department of the Environment v Thomas Bates & Son Ltd (1989)

The defendant building contractor constructed a tower block in Essex, upon completion of which the claimant took possession of the top two floors. Upon undertaking remedial works to the roof, it transpired that the defendant had used low-strength concrete in the pillars with the result that they were incapable of supporting the design load (although they were capable of supporting the existing load). The claimant sought to recover from the defendant sums paid under its lease to its landlord in respect of strengthening works carried out to the pillars, relying on Lord Oliver's judgment in *D&F Estates* as support of its contentions that the remedial work was necessary to prevent an imminent risk of physical injury to persons. However, on the facts, the defects in the pillars did not pose an inevitable danger (on the basis that they were discovered and, as a result, the existing load would not be increased). As such, the claimant's loss (effectively the cost of reinforcing the columns) was purely economic and irrecoverable.

Warner v Basildon Development Corp (1990)

The plaintiff was a subsequent purchaser of a house constructed by the defendant. He brought proceedings in tort for negligently constructing its foundations and relied on the 'complex structure theory'. The court rejected the argument on the basis that the theory was inconsistent with the 'first principles' upon which *D&F Estates* was decided (at 155):

> 'The theory of complex structures – and, I would add, of complex chattels – as a general concept forms, in my judgment, no part of those principles.'

Murphy v Brentwood DC (1991)

Lord Bridge reconsidered what he had said in *D&F Estates*. It was considered that the structural elements in any building form a single indivisible unit of which the different parts are essentially interdependent. To the extent that there is any defect in one part of the structure it must to a greater or lesser degree necessarily affect all the other parts of the structure.

Any defect in the structure should be seen as a defect in the quality of the whole and therefore artificial, in order to impose a legal liability which the law would not otherwise impose, to treat a defect in an integral structure as a defect liable to cause damage to 'other property'.

The House of Lords made clear that a distinction must be drawn between:

'… some part of a complex structure which is said to be a "danger" only because it does not perform its proper function in sustaining the other parts and some distinct item incorporated in the structure which positively malfunctions so as to inflict positive damage on the structure in which it is incorporated'.

The examples given by Lord Bridge were of a defective central heating boiler exploding and damaging a house, or a defective electrical installation malfunctioning and setting a house on fire. In these circumstances, the owner of the house (if he can prove that the damage was due to the negligence of the boiler manufacturer in the one case or the electrical contractor in the other) can recover damages in tort.

However, it was made clear that the position in law is entirely different where, by reason of the inadequacy of the foundations of the building to support the weight of the superstructure, differential settlement and consequent cracking occurs. Once the defect is known the building no longer represents a source of danger.

The court's views in relation to the complex structure theory were therefore that:

- to apply the complex structure theory to a house so that each part of the entire structure is treated as a separate piece of property is likely to be considered unrealistic;

- a builder who builds a house from foundations upwards is creating a single integrated unit of which the individual components are interdependent and to treat the foundations as a piece of property separate from the walls or the floors is artificial;

- the only context for the complex structure theory in the case of a building would be where one integral component of the structure was built by a separate contractor and where a defect in such a component had caused damage to other parts of the structure, e.g.:

  - a steel frame erected by a specialist contractor which failed to give adequate support to floors or walls;

  - defects in ancillary equipment such as central heating boilers or electrical installations;

if such defects gave rise to damage to other parts of the building.

It would seem that the decision of the House of Lords in *Murphy* offers (at best) very equivocal support for the 'complex structure theory'. Indeed, with the exception of defects causing 'positive damage' (such as electrical fire and boiler explosions) as opposed to defects which merely cause a part of a structure to function inadequately, it may well be that the House of Lords intended to sweep the 'complex structure theory' under the carpet altogether. This has not, however, deterred claimants from attempting to rely on it in subsequent cases, with varying degrees of success.

Jacobs v Morton & Partners (1994)

In 1986, owners of a semi-detached house engaged the defendants, a firm of consulting structural engineers, to provide professional advice in respect of cracking caused by ground movement and to design and oversee remedial works to repair the same and to prevent any further cracking occurring. Such works were carried out in 1987 and comprised the construction of a piled raft foundation to underpin the house. In 1988 the plaintiffs acquired the freehold title to the house. Soon after, further cracking occurred which was attributable to heave and the failure of the 1987 remedial works to allow for this. It was common ground that the only way to rectify the damage would be to demolish and rebuild the house.

In his judgment, Mr Recorder Jackson QC held that on a proper interpretation of *Murphy v Brentwood*, the 'complex structure' concept was alive, and went on to set out four factors which would assist in determining whether or not it is applicable in any one particular case:

1 whether the item in question was constructed by someone other than the main contractor responsible for the main building works;

2 whether the item in question has retained its separate identity (for example, a central heating boiler) or whether it has merged with the remainder of the building (for example, a wall);

3   whether the item positively inflicts damage on the building (for example, faulty electrical wiring which causes a fire) or whether it simply fails to perform its function and thus permits damage to occur;

4   whether the item in question was constructed at a different time from the rest of the building (this factor did not arise for consideration in *Murphy v Brentwood*).

The court held that the damage suffered by the plaintiffs was properly characterised as property damage as it fell within the complex structure exception. Significant emphasis was placed on the fact that the raft foundation was constructed some eight years after the house itself.

Tesco Stores Ltd v Norman Hitchcox Partnership & others (1997)

In 1993, a shopping complex in Maidstone was gutted by a fire started deliberately by youths. The fire had spread rapidly through the premises and devastated a supermarket leased by the plaintiff. Proceedings were issued against the defendants (NHP) who had been engaged to design the shopping centre, to complete the design of fit-out works in the supermarket and to supervise the carrying out of the same. The case against NHP was that it failed to design the supermarket so as properly to prevent against the spread of fire and/or that it had failed to supervise the fit-out works during or after its completion.

The court rejected the application of the 'complex structure theory' on the basis that the structures within the building that were intended to prevent the spread of fire could not be said to have malfunctioned so as to have inflicted positive damage on the structure in which they were incorporated. In other words, a failure to install properly fire-stopping mechanisms was not sufficient to fall within one of the complex structure exceptions contemplated in *D&F Estates* and *Murphy v Brentwood*. However, loss arising out of destroyed stock stored on the premises would be recoverable.

Tunnel Refineries v Bryan Donkin Ltd and others (1998)

The defendant was responsible for the design, manufacture and installation of compressors for a syrup production plant owned by the claimant. Within such compressors was a 'rotating assembly' which comprised a fan, radial and shaft. In 1990 one of the fans shattered, destroying the surrounding compressor, but causing no further damage to other property. The judge:

- considered that Lord Bridge's comments in *Murphy v Brentwood* were not binding and, in any event, only went as far as suggesting that the exception for complex structures might 'possibly' apply to complex chattels;

- refused to follow *Jacobs v Morton*, on the basis that he was constrained by the Court of Appeal's decision in *Warner v Basildon* (above, the same not having been cited in *Jacobs v Morton*);

- rejected the argument that the fan had a 'separate identity' from the rest of the compressor, despite the fact that it could be separated and removed for servicing and/or replacement;

- dealt in detail with what he termed the 'demise of the complex chattel exception' and rejected it as 'inconsistent with first principles':

    'In short, when the Fan shattered and wrecked the Compressor, the Compressor was not "other property" for the purpose of the exclusionary rule. The Fan was simply the particular defective part of a defective Compressor.'

Bellefield Computer Services v E Turner & Sons Ltd (2000)

The defendant building contractors were engaged to construct a dairy. The dairy building itself was separated into different areas, namely a storage area, a bottling factory, a laboratory and offices. The storage area was separated from the rest of the premises by a compartment wall which was intended to act as a firebreak. As it turned out, the compartment wall was poorly constructed and failed to contain a fire which broke out in the storage area, causing substantial damage. On appeal, the appellant sought to argue that a distinction should be drawn between the different areas of the building, on account of the different purposes for which each was put to use. The Court of Appeal, following *Murphy v Brentwood*, roundly rejected this argument, holding that:

- the building was constructed and acquired as one unit; and

- as a result, the defendant contractors owed no duty of care as the damage complained of was damage to the 'thing itself'.

Payne v Setchell (2002)

The defendant was a firm of chartered structural and civil engineers who advised the original owners of a property that its long-term structural stability could not be guaranteed. To this end, the defendant recommended the demolition and reconstruction of two new properties on a shared reinforced concrete raft foundation. The claimant was employed to construct the foundations which were inspected and certified as complete by the defendant. Further properties were constructed on the same site and the defendant duly carried out further ground inspections and provided further written certification of the integrity of their foundations. Ownership of one of the properties passed to the claimant. Movement subsequently occurred in all of the properties and the claimant was advised that underpinning was required.

The court held that:

- the 'complex structure theory' was no longer tenable;

- the submission that foundations under one property ought be treated as distinct from those under a different property, where the foundation was shared, was 'artificial' and rejected.

(See also 4.4.1 in relation to this case.)

4.6 RISK OF FUTURE DAMAGE

The above cases deal with scenarios where damage has already occurred. But what is the position when a party seeks to sue another to prevent *future* damage from occurring?

Midland Bank plc v Bardgrove Property Services Ltd (1992)

The plaintiff bank occupied premises next to a construction site being developed by the first defendant. In carrying out excavation works, the second defendants, a firm of contractors, exposed a vertical earth wall along the boundary with the bank's premises. Despite temporary measures being implemented to shore up the earth wall, subsidence occurred. Damage was caused to the bank's property and such damage was put right by the defendants.

The bank, in order to prevent the risk of any further rotational ground failure (but despite the fact that no further movement had actually occurred) sank sheet piles into its land at a cost of £230,000. Proceedings were issued to recover the cost of such works.

The Court of Appeal held that actual physical damage was required in order to recover in the tort of interference with a neighbour's right to lateral support of land. The claim failed; the steps taken by the bank were to prevent future damage. However, the court would have been willing to grant a mandatory injunction to carry out works to minimise or eradicate the risk of future rotational failure had the claimant applied for one.

However, it appears that when suing in negligence, and where a 'special relationship' is present, recovery in respect of future damage will be permissible.

Murphy v Brentwood DC (1991)

In commenting on the decision in *Pirelli v Oscar Faber* (discussed at 4.3 above), Lord Keith (at 466) suggested that there may indeed be circumstances in which a party has a cause of action in tort even though physical damage had not yet occurred:

> 'If the plaintiffs had happened to discover the defect before any damage had occurred there would seem to be no good reason for holding that they would not have had a cause of action in tort at that stage, *without having to wait until some damage had occurred*. They would have suffered economic loss through having a defective chimney on which they required to spend money for the purpose of removing the defect.' (Emphasis added.)

4.6.1 Summary

- Even though a building may contain design or workmanship defects, it does not necessarily follow that a party will have suffered 'damage' recoverable in tort as a result of such defects.

- Absent a contract or a 'special relationship' between the parties, it is essential that the loss complained of has *not* resulted from the structure or chattel damaging itself. Such loss is 'purely economic' and is irrecoverable.

- The so-called 'complex structure' or 'complex chattel' theory raised by the House of Lords in *D&F Estates* attempts to avoid this restriction. However:

  - whilst it has not been expressly rejected by the House of Lords, recent decisions of the lower courts suggest that it is largely unsustainable;

  - *D&F Estates* is frequently distinguished on the facts;

  - the complex structure theory may be relevant in limited circumstances, such as those considered in *Jacobs v Morton & Partners*.

- Absent a contract or a 'special relationship' between the parties, recovery for the risk of future damage is impermissible, although an injunction may be sought to prevent such damage occurring.

5
The Defective Premises Act 1972

5.1 INTRODUCTION

The *Defective Premises Act* 1972 ('the DPA 1972') is relevant where the defect is such that the premises will not be fit for habitation. Whilst therefore it does not apply to all defects, it remains an important weapon if a dwelling is substantially defective but where there is no direct cause of action (e.g. through contract).

5.2 THE DUTY TO BUILD DWELLINGS PROPERLY

Defective Premises Act 1972, s. 1(1)

'A person taking on work for or in connection with the provision of a dwelling (whether the dwelling is provided by the erection or by the conversion or enlargement of a building) owes a duty:

(a) if the dwelling is provided to the order of any person, to that person; and

(b) without prejudice to paragraph (a) above, to every person who acquires an interest (whether legal or equitable) in the dwelling;

to see that the work which he takes on is done in a workmanlike or, as the case may be, professional manner, with proper materials and so that as regards that work the dwelling will be fit for habitation when completed.'

5.2.1 'Taking on work ...'

Alexander v Mercouris (1979)

The plaintiffs brought proceedings against the defendants claiming that they were in breach of their duty under s. 1 of the DPA 1972. Buckley LJ held that the duty was one to be performed during the carrying on of the work. Thus, if, at an early stage in the provision of the dwelling – for instance, the putting in of the foundations – someone who had taken on that part of the work failed to do it in a workmanlike manner, then an immediate cause of action would arise. It would not be necessary to await the completion of the dwelling to claim relief on the basis of a breach of statutory duty. [This is obviously inconsistent with any argument that, in relation to a particular defect, there is merely a temporary disconformity and therefore no breach: see Chapter 3.]

The case also decided that the Act was intended to apply not only to cases in which a contractual obligation to work exists, but also to cases in which the work may be done without contractual obligation but in circumstances in which he who does the work could claim reward on the basis of a quantum meruit, to cases in which the work is done voluntarily without expectation of gain and, perhaps most importantly, to cases in which a building owner does the work himself.

Sparham-Souter v Town & Country Developments (Essex) Ltd (1976)

Whilst not ultimately settled, it is doubtful that the DPA 1972 gives a remedy against a local authority, whose inspector is negligent or turns a blind eye in relation to the passing of defective plans. It depends on whether he 'takes on work in connection with' the provision of the house. Denning MR considered that those words may give rise to much debate, even up to the House of Lords.

[*Sparham Souter* was subsequently overruled in *Pirelli General Cable Works Ltd v Oscar Faber & Partners* in relation to a different point.]

5.3 MEANING OF 'DWELLING'

'Dwelling' is not defined within the DPA 1972.

Campbell v O'Sullivan (1947)

'"Dwelling" ordinarily signifies a place of abode or residence, a tenement, habitation, or house, which premises a person or persons are using as a place fore sleeping, and usually for the provision of some or all of their meals. The word is not used as a term of art, and has to be interpreted with its ordinary, proper and grammatical sense in the context in which it appears ...'

Housing Act 1985 ss. 237, 525

'"dwelling" means a building or part of a building occupied or intended to be occupied as a separate dwelling, together with any yard, garden, outhouses and appurtenances belonging to it or usually enjoyed with it;'.

5.3.1 '... the provision of a dwelling ...'

Jacobs v Morton & Partners (1994)

This phrase connotes the creation of a new dwelling. It does not include rectification of an existing dwelling. This is because:

- in ordinary usage the word 'provision' refers to the initial supply of an item;

- the phrase in brackets in the second and third lines of s. 1(1) appears to be directed to the creation of new dwellings, either by construction or by adaptation;

- if parliament had intended to include works of rectification within the ambit of s. 1, it would have said so expressly.

5.4 THE NATURE OF THE DUTY

Alexander v Mercouris (1979)

(The facts of this case are set out at 5.2.1 above.) The reference to the dwelling being fit for habitation indicated the intended consequence of the proper performance of the duty and provides a measure of the standard of the requisite work and materials.

Thompson v Clive Alexander & Partners (1992)

It is necessary for a claimant to prove that the defect rendered the dwelling unfit for habitation since fitness for habitation was a measure of the standard required in the performance of the duty imposed by s. 1(1). It is not reasonable to construe s. 1(1) of the DPA 1972 in a way which could make the builders or designers of a dwelling liable to a person who was not even the original purchaser for trivial defects in its design, construction or in the materials used which did not render it fit for habitation. The existence of such defects would in many cases, if not all, be reflected in the price paid by a person acquiring an interest in the dwelling.

Andrews v Schooling (1991)

The plaintiff purchased a leasehold interest in a flat with a cellar. Extensive works had been carried out in converting the property to a flat, but the only work carried out to the cellar was the painting of the walls. The flat suffered from penetrating dampness which the plaintiff alleged emanated from the cellar and by a writ she claimed damages from the first to third defendants for breach of duty under s. 1 of the DPA 1972. It was held that s. 1 of the DPA 1972 applies to a case of non-feasance as well as to cases of misfeasance, so that a dwelling was unfit for habitation for the purpose of s. 1 where it was without some essential attribute on completion of the works, though the problems arising therefrom had not then become patent. The penetrating dampness, on the facts, rendered the flat not fit for habitation.

Smith v Drumm (1996)

The vendor of a recently converted flat had employed others to connect the gas and electricity. Nevertheless he had 'taken on work' within the meaning of s. 1(1) of the DPA 1972, and this section did not only apply to work completed but also to work omitted.

Mirza v Baljit S Bhandal (1999)

It was held that the purpose of the duty imposed was to ensure that the dwelling should be fit for habitation. The 'work' referred to was therefore the overall scheme. In *Mirza*, the scheme was the rebuilding of a dwelling and it was necessary to design, construct and inspect the scheme in a professional manner. The duty was not to be restricted to the specific instructions given to those individually taking on aspects of the work, or else a person could avoid liability by failing to instruct a workman where the services of that workman were required to complete the scheme properly.

5.5 'FIT FOR HABITATION'

Bayoumi v Protim Services Ltd (1996)

The defendant's argument that unless its breach was the only cause of the property's unfitness for habitation it could not be liable under the DPA 1972, failed. The true test was whether the breach was a significant cause of, or factor in, the property's unfitness.

Johnson v Sheffield County Council (1994)

The court held that the 'fitness standard' pursuant to s. 604 of the *Housing Act* 1985 can be used as a checklist for consideration of fitness for habitation. This case preceded the replacement of the fitness standard in the *Housing Act* 2004, which introduced a 'Housing Health and Safety Rating System' (HHSRS). The concept of unfitness within the *Housing Act* will be replaced by an assessment as to the extent to which a house is free from hazards to health and safety. The HHSRS places the emphasis on the occupant, rather than the building.

However, it is thought that for the purposes of actions brought under the DPA 1972, where it is a necessary ingredient to demonstrate that a defect gives rise to the property being unfit for habitation, the 'fitness standard' will remain a useful guide. The relevant criteria for fitness are that the property:

- is structurally stable: any permissible movement must be of such a degree as to not constitute a threat to the occupants (see *Jennings v Tavener*, below);

- is free from dampness prejudicial to the health of the occupants (if any): dampness will only constitute unfitness if it is serious and prejudicial to health;

- has adequate provision for lighting, heating and ventilation (see *Nottingham Community Housing Association Ltd v Powerminster Ltd*):
  - adequate natural lighting (under good weather conditions) should be available in rooms intended for sleeping, sitting or eating meals. A usual test for this is whether a newspaper can be read in all parts of the room without the aid of artificial light;
  - ventilation should be sufficient to provide one air change per hour in habitable rooms and up to three in bathrooms and toilets;
  - adequate provision for heating means that it is necessary to provide a suitably located gas or electric point (see *Smith v Drumm*);

- has an adequate piped supply of wholesome water:
  - this relates to both the quality of the water and the speed of flow;
  - has satisfactory facilities for the preparation and cooking of food, including a sink with a satisfactory supply of hot and cold water: an inconvenient layout of a kitchen will not constitute unfitness unless it is actually dangerous;

- has a suitably located water-closet for the exclusive use of the occupants (if any): there must be adequate ventilation and the toilet should be sufficiently accessible at all times without compromising the privacy of the occupants;

- has a suitably located fixed bath or shower and wash-hand basin each of which is provided with a satisfactory supply of hot and cold water: it should be cleanable, ventilated and sufficiently accessible;
- has an effective system for the draining of foul, waste and surface water. Factors taken into account include:
  - the capacity of the system;
  - susceptibility to leakages or blockages; and
  - whether foul air from sewage can enter the dwelling.

Batty v Metropolitan Property Realisations Ltd (1978)

At some time not later than ten years after the date of the trial, possibly much earlier, the movement of the strata on the hillside on the slopes adjacent to the plaintiffs' house would cause the foundations of that house to slide down the hill and the house would be in ruins. At the date of trial, the house was already unsaleable. The only defect was the nature of the land on which the house relied for its support. It was unstable, and by its instability the house was, from the outset, doomed. Thus, for that reason, the house was unfit for human habitation, because in a foreseeable (and short) time it would collapse, through the movement of the hillside.

[In *D&F Estates v Church Commissioners for England and others* (1989), this decision was questioned by Lord Bridge (who had himself given the judgment in *Batty*) as being 'unsound' but remains useful for illustration on the facts.]

Nottingham Community Housing Association Ltd v Powerminster Ltd (2000)

Lighting, power supply, drainage, sanitation and water supply are all vital parts of a building, whose proper functioning is required if a building is to be fit for habitation.

Smith v Drumm (1996)

(The facts of this case are set out at 5.4 above.) The vendor of a recently converted flat was in breach of the DPA 1972 because without the supply of gas (which had not been connected) and electricity (which had been disconnected because the fuse box was illegal) the flat had not been fit for habitation.

Mirza v Baljit S Bhandal (1999)

(The facts of this case are set out at 5.4 above.) The dwelling had not been fit for habitation when completed because the inadequacy of the foundations was inevitably going to produce a situation in which the house would collapse. Such a house was not 'fit for habitation when completed'.

Sleafer v Lambeth Borough Council (1960)

The door was faulty, partly because one of its sides was binding at the bottom against the jamb, and partly because the weather board at the foot of the door was binding on the floor underneath. It was considered to be the simplest possible operation to put such a door into proper repair, and was not regarded as anything other than a very trivial repair. The tenant was leaving his flat by the front door when, owing to the defect, he had to use force to close the door by pulling on the only external handle, the letter-box knocker. The knocker came off and he fell backwards against an iron balustrade and suffered injury to his back. Whilst it did not have to decide the issue, the Court of Appeal doubted whether the trivial defect would render the property unfit for habitation.

Stanton v Southwick (1920)

The case was fought upon the footing that rats had their home in the sewer passing below the house, and that from the sewer they made incursions into the house in search of food. The Court of Appeal decided that the presence in the house of the rats to that extent did not breach an obligation that the property be fit for habitation.

Miller v Cannon Hill Estates Ltd (1931)

Serious damp penetrated a house during the winter. The plaintiff, acting on medical advice, left the house. The house was not fit for habitation by reason of the damp.

Summers v Salford Corporation (1941)

A sash-cord of the only window in one of the bedrooms within a flat broke, and the window stuck. While the plaintiff was cleaning the window, the other sash-cord broke, her hand was jammed between the two parts of the window and she was severely injured. The breaking of the sash-cord did not render the house unfit for human habitation.

Jennings v Tavener (1955)

Soon after the plaintiffs occupied a bungalow, cracks appeared in the walls, and other cracks developed later. The cracks were caused by the withdrawal of moisture from the site by the roots of poplar trees growing in a cemetery some 30 or 40 feet from the back of the bungalow. The obligation that works should be carried out during the course of construction so that it should be fit for habitation was not confined to the parts of the house above the ground, but extended to the provision of proper foundations on ground where they would not settle. The cracks, caused by the subsidence, rendered the house not fit for habitation.

5.6 PERSONS OWING THE DUTY

Section 1(4) of the DPA 1972 provides:

'A person who:

(a) in the course of a business which consists of or includes providing or arranging for the provision of dwellings or installations in dwellings; or

(b) in the exercise of a power of making such provision or arrangements conferred by or by virtue of any enactment;

arranges for another to take on work for or in connection with the provision of a dwelling shall be treated for the purposes of this section as included among the persons who have taken on the work.'

Mirza v Baljit S Bhandal (1999)

(The facts of this case are set out at 5.4 above.) This claim arose out of the subsidence of an end of terrace house, which the claimant bought from the defendant and his mother and father, who were then trading in partnership which, at least on this occasion, carried out the conversion and resale of this dwelling. The partnership had given instructions to others, including an architect. It was held that an 'owner' was included in s. 1(1) of the DPA 1972, provided that it could be said that he had 'taken on' work in relation to the building. The owner of a dwelling did not 'take on work' merely by giving instructions for work to be done. However, because the partnership was in the business of arranging for the provision of at least this dwelling, the partnership owed a duty under s. 1(4) of the Act. The use of the word 'dwellings' in the plural in s. 1(4) did not exclude a one-off activity. A business need not have provided for more than one dwelling.

5.7 THE DEFENCE OF INSTRUCTION

Section 1(2) and (3) of the DPA 1972 provides:

'(2) A person who takes on any such work for another on terms that he is to do it in accordance with instructions given by or on behalf of that other shall, to the extent to which he does it properly in accordance with those instructions, be treated for the purposes of this section as discharging the duty imposed on him by subsection (1) above except where he owes a duty to that other to warn him of any defects in the instructions and fails to discharge that duty.

(3) A person shall not be treated for the purposes of subsection (2) above as having given instructions for the doing of work merely because he has agreed to the work being done in a specified manner, with specified materials or to a specified design.'

Thus, a contrast is anticipated between those who have merely agreed that works can be carried out in a certain way (as for example, an employer agreeing to contractor's proposals as part of the contract) and the giving of instructions. This will be a question of fact in each case.

Mirza v Baljit S Bhandal (1999)

(The facts of this case are set out at 5.4 above.) The instructions given did not amount to a defence under s. 1(2).

Instead, they constituted an arrangement of others to take on work for the purposes of s. 1(4). This, however, is because the instructions were given by a business which was arranging for the provision of dwellings.

5.8 MEASURE OF LOSS

Bayoumi v Protim Services Ltd (1996)

Damages under the DPA 1972 should cover all losses which were the natural consequence of the breach, and not reflect merely either the cost of repair or diminution. The plaintiff was therefore entitled to a sum for loss of use and enjoyment of the property (although a claim for lack of rental income failed on the facts).

6
The surveyor's duty to identify defects

6.1 INTRODUCTION

This chapter is concerned with those cases in which the surveyor's duties which relate to the identification or valuation of defects have been explored. The numerous wider issues arising out of valuers and surveyors negligence (for example, duty of care, loss and contributory negligence) are the topic of a separate book (see *Case in Point – Negligence in Valuations and Surveys* by John Murdoch). The most common complaint against surveyors is a failure to have identified defects in the subject property.

6.2 THE IDENTIFICATION OF DEFECTS

A failure to have identified a defect in itself does not amount to negligence. In each case the court will ask itself whether, given the nature of the inspection and the nature of the defect, a reasonably competent surveyor would have discovered it.

Smith v Eric S Bush (1990)

The House of Lords considered that the valuer must be a professional person, typically a chartered surveyor in general practice, who, by training and experience and exercising reasonable skill and care, will recognise defects and be able to assess value. The valuer should value the house after taking into consideration major defects which are, or ought to be, obvious to him, in the course of a visual inspection of so much of the exterior and interior of the house as may be accessible to him without undue difficulty.

6.2.1 The nature of the inspection

The extent to which defects should be identified by the surveyor will depend upon the nature of the inspection being carried out. There are three principle levels of inspection:

- *A mortgage valuation.* This is the most basic survey which will involve carrying out such visual inspection as is reasonably practicable to report anything so material as would or might influence the value of the property.
- *An RICS Homebuyer Survey.* This is prepared on a pre-printed form prepared by the Royal Institution of Chartered Surveyors. Each element of the property should be inspected, although the level of reporting detail is slightly less than would be required in a building survey.
- *A building survey (often called a structural survey).* This is meant to be a comprehensive and detailed report on the current condition of the property and should take several hours to prepare. Each visible element of the property is inspected to ascertain its condition and suitability, any necessary repairs will be identified as will anticipated major expenditure, such as the replacement of the roof or wiring.

Stewart v H A Brechin & Co (1959)

The court held that 'anything of significance' in the context of a valuation meant anything so material as would or might influence a reasonable person in fixing a price to be offered, or anything which to the skilled eye of a surveyor would be an indication of possible and material defect, structural or otherwise, such as would, or might reasonably, be expected to affect its value to a prospective purchaser or cause reconsideration of an intention to make an offer for the property. The defendant surveyor was held negligent for having failed to discover significant woodworm infestation. He should have inspected the roofspaces of an old manorhouse and its outbuildings.

Cross v David Martin & Mortimer (1984)

Notwithstanding the more limited scope of a homebuyer survey, the court found that a surveyor who is instructed to carry out such an inspection should show the same level of expertise as is required for a full survey.

6.2.2 The extent of the inspection

Roberts v Hampson & Co (1988)

The court considered that:

> 'Both the expert surveyors who gave evidence before me agreed that with a house of this size they would allow about half-an-hour for their inspection on site. That time does not admit of moving furniture, or of lifting carpets, especially where they are nailed down. In my judgment, it must be accepted that where a surveyor undertakes a scheme valuation it is understood that he is making a limited appraisal only. It is, however, an appraisal by a skilled professional man. It is inherent in any standard fee work that some cases will colloquially be "winners" and others "losers", from the professional man's point of view. The fact that in an individual case he may need to spend two or three times as long as he would have expected, or as the fee structure would have contemplated, is something which he must accept.'

Hill v Debenham, Tewson and Chinnocks (1958)

The defendant surveyor was held negligent in failing to give a warning in relation to the rafters and the battens, which would need replacing. The court held that the surveyor either should have climbed up a ladder in the valley between the two roofs to inspect the rafters by gaps in the tiles, or stated that he did not know what the state of the rafters and battens was.

Conn v Munday (1955)

An apparent failure to have discovered woodworm in the cellar of a house led to a finding of negligence on the part of the surveyor.

Drinnan v C W Ingram & Sons (1967)

A surveyor who is valuing one flat within a block would be required to have at least some regard to the structure of the building as a whole. In the absence of precise instructions to do so, a surveyor would not be bound to make a meticulous examination of the whole of the building, but normal practice should have regard to anything clearly visible in the structure.

Bishop v Watson, Watson & Scoles (1972)

Absent a specific agreement to do so, a surveyor carrying out a visual survey would be under no obligation to uncover those parts of the building where the flashings or damp proof courses should be found to see if they are there and, if so, whether they are adequate. If the surveyor sees anything which would give a reasonably skilled person grounds to suspect that the flashings or damp proof course are missing or inadequate, he must draw his client's attention to the matter. Evidence that the building is of cavity construction is not of itself ground for suspecting that the safeguards essential to that mode of construction have been omitted or botched.

6.2.3 The nature of the defect

Fisher v Knowles (1982)

The court considered that, in the context of the identification of defects in a survey, the word 'defect' may mean different things:

> 'The word "defect" is a word having a number of connotations. Defects may be something which is inherent in the type and age of a building. For example, an Elizabethan cottage is likely to have the defect of having low ceilings, a defect both in the ordinary sense and in the statutory sense. To some people, though, that would be considered to be an enhancement. There are defects of some kind in every home. There are creaking floorboards, gaps between the wainscot and the floor. There are cracks in the ceilings. One would be very lucky indeed to buy even a new house, let alone a 25 year old house as this one without finding some cracks in the ceiling.'

In considering the claims, the court took account of those defects which were of such a nature that a prudent person would have put right and which would have been apparent to the defendant, taking into account the type and age of the property.

6.2.4 The trail of suspicion

The test will always be whether a reasonably competent surveyor should have identified the defect in question, in the context of the investigation being carried out. This may, however, include the identification of 'hidden' defects which would have been discoverable by the reasonably competent surveyor following a trail of suspicion.

Roberts v Hampson & Co (1988)

(The facts of this case are set out at 6.2.2 above.) The surveyor's report drew attention to some dampness in the external walls and some dry rot in the skirting board of one of the bedrooms. The property was in fact subject to serious dry rot infestation. The court considered that if a surveyor misses a defect because its signs are hidden, that is a risk which is to be accepted by the client. However, if there is a specific ground for suspicion and that trail leads to lifting carpets or looking behind furniture, the surveyor must take reasonable steps to follow the trail until he has all the information which it is reasonable for him to have before making his valuation.

[In *Smith v Bush* (see 6.2 above) the House of Lords also expressly approved the court's judgment in *Roberts v Hampson*.]

Hipkins v Jack Cotton Partnership (1989)

A surveyor was found negligent for failing to observe cracking and patching in the rendering of a wall, which were the clues to a structural defect in the foundations which a reasonably competent surveyor would not have missed, nor have failed to ask himself why they were there.

Hardy v Wamsley-Lewis (1967)

The defendant surveyor failed to identify dry rot 'waviness' in the skirting board between the front door and the staircase.

This of itself may not have been sufficient to establish negligence, but he also concluded that dry rot identified on a doorpost was dormant. This being so, he should have meticulously examined every bit of wood he could see to see if there were signs of it spreading at all.

Cross v David Martin & Mortimer (1989)

(The facts of this case are set out at 6.2.1 above.) The surveyor failed to notice and consider the significance of a hump in the hall floor. Together with other indicators, this should have alerted the surveyor to the possibility of subsidence.

Hacker v Thomas Deal & Co (1991)

The court accepted the evidence of an expert that although a surveyor is acting as a detective, one does not start going into all the little crevices in the hopes of finding something unless there is some telltale sign which indicates that it would be advisable to do so.

Ker v John H Allan & Son (1949)

The court considered that the presence of dry rot ought always to be in the mind of a surveyor and that he should always be on the look out for any evidence that might be suggestive of dry rot. However, in the absence of any suspicious circumstances his duty does not require him to cause carpets and linoleum to be lifted and to go underneath floors and make a detailed examination of every hidden corner of a building.

Hingorani v Blower (1976)

The trail of suspicion may be aroused by recent redecoration or repairs. In this case the court found that the surveyor should have been aware of a filled-in external crack which was a clue to structural defects within the property.

6.2.5 Reporting of the defect

Oswald v Countrywide Surveyors Ltd (1996)

It was negligent in a report of a survey in an old timber-framed house not to distinguish between infestation by common furniture beetle and infestation by death watch beetle.

6.3 CONSEQUENCES OF FAILING TO IDENTIFY DEFECTS

A comprehensive review of the case law relating to causation and loss arising out of a surveyor's negligence for failing to identify defects is outside the scope of this book (see *Case in Point – Negligence in Valuations and Surveys* by John Murdoch). However, of particular interest is *Baxall*, set out below, which relates to the relationship between an architect's liability for a design defect and a surveyor's liability for failing to identify it.

(1) Baxall Securities Ltd (2) Norbain Sdc Ltd v (1) Sheard Walshaw Partnership (2) Shaw Whitmore Partnership (3) Birse Construction Ltd (4) Fk Roofing Ltd (5) Fullflow Ltd (2002)

The claim concerned an industrial unit, designed by the first defendants (SWP). It was defective in that the gutter ought to have had, but did not have, overflows. Prior to entering into a tenancy agreement in relation to the unit, the claimants (B) instructed surveyors (LSH) to inspect the building. LSH failed to detect the absence of overflows. Owing to the inability of the gutter and its associated drainage system to cope with the heavy rainfall, the building flooded, damaging the claimants' goods. The Court of Appeal found:

- if in the normal course of events, a surveyor would be engaged in a survey of a building for a purchaser and, with the exercise of due diligence, that surveyor would have discovered a defect, the defect was to be treated as patent;

- this would be so whether or not a surveyor had in fact been engaged and, if engaged, whether or not the surveyor had performed his task competently;

- in an action against SWP to recover the value of the goods damaged, SWP successfully argued that LSH's failure to have detected the absence of overflows was a break in the chain of causation.

Whilst not an issue in the case, it follows from the second finding above that:

- if LSH had been sued in relation to the damage caused by the defective gutter, they would have been found liable;
- if LSH had sought a contribution from SWP pursuant to the *Civil Liability (Contribution) Act* 1978, the action would have failed given that SWP was not liable to B;
- accordingly, a negligent failure by a surveyor to identify a patent defect may result in the surveyor being liable for all the consequences of the existence of the defect, and the effective absolution of the original negligent designer.

7

Defects and limitation periods

7.1 INTRODUCTION

There are strict timeframes within which proceedings must be issued. The logic behind this is that whilst it is right that a party must, in broad terms at least, be responsible should its construction works be defective, he should not hold himself open for an indefinite period of time to answer a stale claim. The timeframes in question have been fixed by Parliament since 1623 and are currently set out in the *Limitation Act* 1980.

Different rules may apply in the event that defects (or the consequences of defects) manifest themselves outside of the primary 'limitation period' or if a party has deliberately or recklessly concealed such defects from the other. Such scenarios are considered in more detail below.

7.2 LIMITATION FOR BREACH OF CONTRACT

Limitation Act 1980, ss. 5, 8

'**5. Time limit for actions founded on simple contract**

An action founded on simple contract shall not be brought after the expiration of six years from the date on which the cause of action accrued.

…

8. Time limits for actions on a specialty [including a contract under seal]

(1) An action upon a specialty shall not be brought after the expiration of twelve years from the date on which the cause of action accrued.

(2) Subsection (1) above shall not affect any action for which a shorter period of limitation is prescribed by any other provision of this Act.'

7.2.1 Cause of action is usually breach of contract

Gibbs v Guild (1881)

That a party's cause of action will accrue at the time of breach of contract is a long-standing principle of English law which dates back to the 'action of assumpsit'. It is the breach of contract which is the 'gist of the action'; consequently, time will run from the date of such a breach.

New Islington and Hackney Housing Association Ltd v Pollard Thomas and Edwards Ltd (2001)

The defendants were appointed in 1990 as architects in respect of the design and construction of six properties on various sites acquired by the claimant housing authority. Soon after the works were practically complete (between February and March 1992) and the properties occupied, the claimant became aware of numerous complaints from residents concerning noise. The claimant brought proceedings on 1 May 1998 for breach of contract and negligence, claiming that the defendants' defective design failed to incorporate adequate soundproofing between flats in the properties.

Dyson J held that upon a proper construction of the contract and of the defendants' terms and conditions of engagement, it could not be said that the defendants were under a duty to review the adequacy of design (an in particular the adequacy of sound insulation) after practical completion had taken place. Consequently, breach took place before 1 May 1992, and proceedings were dismissed.

Chapman v Gwyther (1866)

In a contract for the sale of a horse pursuant to which the defendant warranted the horse as 'sound for a month', the court held that the defendant would be answerable for any defects in the horse which came to light during that period.

7.2.2 Summary

- The ordinary time limit in which a party must bring a claim is six years from the date of breach of the contract.

- If a contract is under seal then the time limit will be 12 years from the date of its breach.

- It may be that a specific term of a contract warrants or guarantees the durability of the goods or works in question for a period beyond the time limits laid down by statute. In such circumstances, an action for breach of warranty may properly be brought by reference to the extended period.

- The position is different where defects have been deliberately concealed. This is discussed below.

7.3 LIMITATION FOR BREACH OF STATUTORY DUTY UNDER THE DEFECTIVE PREMISES ACT 1972

Defective Premises Act 1972, s. 1(5)

'(5) Any cause of action in respect of a breach of the duty imposed by this section shall be deemed ... to have accrued at a time when the dwelling was completed, but if after that time a person who has done work for or in connection with the provision of the dwelling does further work to rectify the work he has already done, any such cause of action in respect of that further work shall be deemed for those purposes to have accrued at the time when the further work was finished.'

Alderson v Beetham Organisation Ltd (2003)

The defendants were property developers who were responsible for converting a building into flats in 1994. The claimant purchased a long leasehold interest in one of the flats in 1995. Soon after occupation, it was discovered that the flat was susceptible to damp. Remedial works – consisting of the relaying of floor slabs and the fitting of extra drainage – were undertaken by the defendants in 1995 but were ineffective. It transpired that this was because the root cause of the problems was the failure of the damp-proofing system. The claimant brought an action under the *Defective Premises*

Act 1972 ('the DPA 1972' – see generally Chapter 5 above) in 2001, claiming that the defendants had breached their statutory duty to render the property fit for human habitation. The defendants argued that the claim was statute-barred: whilst a new cause of action accrued in 1995 in respect of the remedial works (i.e. the floor slabs and extra drainage), no new cause of action in respect of the original works (i.e. the damp-proofing) arose.

The Court of Appeal rejected the defendants' contentions, and held that in cases where a party has come back to repair a defect but failed to repair it properly, a fresh cause of action accrues at the time of the failed remedial works. In the circumstances, the claim was allowed.

7.4 LIMITATION IN NEGLIGENCE ACTIONS

Limitation Act 1980, s. 2

'2. Time limit for actions founded on tort

An action founded on tort shall not be brought after the expiration of six years from the date on which the cause of action accrued.'

7.4.1 Cause of action accrues on the date that damage occurs

Pirelli General Cable Works Ltd v Oscar Faber & Partners (1983)

The defendant consulting engineers were employed by the claimant to advise on the design of a chimney which was subsequently built in 1969. It transpired that the design was defective in that it provided for inappropriate materials to be incorporated into the structure, and expert evidence determined that cracking, which was not actually discovered until 1977, manifested itself no later than 1970. With reasonable diligence, the claimant could have been expected to have discovered the cracking in 1972. Proceedings were issued in 1978; the defendant contended the same were time-barred.

The House of Lords held that a cause of action in tort accrues on the date of the damage itself, not from the date upon when such damage was discovered or ought reasonably to have been discovered. Consequently, the claimant's case was time-barred as the writ was served more than six years after 1970.

(See also 4.3 in relation to this case.)

7.4.2 Establishing the 'date of damage'

In *Pirelli* (see 7.4.1 above), the court considered that in some circumstances, the date of damage might well occur upon completion of a building if it is so manifestly defective that it is 'doomed from the start' (at 16, 18):

> 'There may perhaps be cases where the defect is so gross that the building is doomed from the start, and where the owner's cause of action will accrue as soon as it is built, but it seems unlikely that such a defect would not be discovered within the limitation period. Such cases, if they exist, would be exceptional.
>
> ... except perhaps where the advice of an architect or consulting engineer leads to the erection of a building which is so defective as to be doomed from the start, the cause of action arises only when physical damage occurs to the building.'

Ketteman v Hansel Properties Ltd (1985)

In 1975 the claimant homeowners purchased houses built by the defendant builders. The following year, cracking occurred which was discovered to be attributable to settlement of the foundations, which had been laid pursuant to an architect's designs between 1973 and 1975. Rather than suffer the inconvenience of underpinning works, the claimants decided to sell their properties at a loss. The architect was joined as a defendant in 1982 when the financial viability of the defendant builders was called into question.

The architect sought to argue that the claim against it was out of time on the grounds that the houses were 'doomed from the start': the plans and siting being faulty, the foundations were bound to settle and cause damage.

The Court of Appeal rejected this argument, following *Pirelli* and holding that the cause of action accrued on the date of the cracking (i.e. in 1976). Only in very exceptional cases will a building be 'doomed from the start'. Consequently, the proceedings were brought timeously.

London Congregational Union v Harriss & Harriss (1988)

The defendant, a firm of architects, was retained by the claimant to design and oversee building works to construct a new church hall. During the course of such works, the contractor omitted to fit a damp-proof course, an omission which was not picked up on by the defendant. Final completion occurred in 1970. Between 1971 and 1975 the building flooded on several occasions as a result of defectively designed drains, and further damage was caused to the blockwork of the hall from water ingress a result of the missing damp-proof course. Proceedings were issued against the defendant in 1978. The defendant argued that the cause of action accrued at the time of erection and/or practical completion of the building, as: (i) the defective drain design was the 'damage' to the property, or (ii) the property was 'doomed from the start' (see commentary on *Pirelli* at 7.4.1 above).

The Court of Appeal held that limitation ran from the date that water damage was caused to the building and the claim was not statute-barred. The design of the drains and the missing damp-proof course were examples of defects which, although causative of the water ingress, did not constitute actionable damage in tort in themselves. The court suggested that there may be circumstances where a defect could constitute actual physical damage to the building, but only where such defects were immediately causative of damage. Even if such damage was inevitable, this is still not sufficient to ground a cause of action. In the circumstances, the drains had been functional for almost two years.

Nitrigin Eireann Teoranta v Inco Alloys Ltd (1992)

This case concerned an explosion in a chemical plant following the escape of methane gas from a pipe supplied by the defendants. The gas escaped from a crack in a section of pipework in 1984, but the same section had in fact cracked (but was repaired) in 1983. Proceedings were not issued until 1990. The defendants argued that limitation ran from the time of the first incidence of cracking (i.e. in 1983) with the result that the proceedings were time-barred.

The court held that the first incidence of cracking, being damage to the pipe itself, constituted 'pure economic loss' (as opposed to damage to 'other' property) and thus no cause of action arose. However, the later incidence of cracking was causative of physical damage to 'other' property (i.e. to the plant surrounding the pipe), and a cause of action first accrued when this actionable damage occurred. Consequently, proceedings had been brought in time.

Nykredit Mortgage Bank plc v Edward Erdman Group Ltd (1997)

On the strength of a valuation report supplied by the defendants, the claimant bank agreed to advance £2.45m to a borrower in respect of a property. The defendants represented that the value of the property was in the region of £3.5m. In actual fact, it transpired that the true value of the property at the time of the valuation was closer to £2m.

The claimant argued that had it been made aware of this at the time, it would not have agreed to advance such a high sum to the borrower, who in the meantime had defaulted on mortgage repayments, obliging the claimant to take possession of the property and sell it. The price achieved at sale was £345,000. The claimant issued proceedings against the defendant in both contract and tort.

The House of Lords held that a cause of action accrued when the claimant first sustained 'measurable relevant loss'. This was deemed to be at or around the time the mortgage was granted. The bank suffered actual loss almost immediately as the borrower had defaulted straight away on repayments and, further, at all times the bank's loan had exceeded the true value of the property.

Havenledge Ltd v Graeme John & Partners (2000)

This case illustrates the difficulty the courts have had in establishing the 'date of damage'. Whilst there was no dispute that the relevant test to apply was when the injured party suffered actual (as opposed to potential or prospective) loss or damage of a kind recognised by law, all three judges arrived at different conclusions as to when such loss was suffered. By a majority of two to one, the claim was allowed to proceed.

The claimants purchased a property in 1987 for the purposes of refurbishing and converting the same into a nursing home. The defendants were a firm of solicitors who negligently failed to advise the claimants to obtain a mining engineer's report in respect of the property prior to purchase.

Over the next five years, mining operations were carried out within influencing distance of the property. Cracks began to appear prior to February 1990 but were not discovered until August 1990. Extensive remedial works were undertaken between 1990 and 1994 and paid for by British Coal.

The claimants alleged that following the discovery of the cracks in August 1990, the nursing home ceased to be a viable business concern and was forced to close down. The claimants brought proceedings in February 1996 to recover losses incurred as a result of the business going into receivership. The three different analyses were:

- The 'relevant loss' was the lost business investment and the financial consequences of the disruption to the business. On the facts, this was not suffered until the date of the discovery of the cracks in August 1990, as it was from such discovery that interference to the business began. Consequently, proceedings were issued in time.

- The 'relevant loss' was the expenditure of sums on the conversion of the property into a nursing home. That expenditure (which was, of course, part of the business investment) was 'abortive' as the property was unsuitable for use as a nursing home. Time ran from when such moneys were first spent, which was within the limitation period.

- The 'relevant loss' was being burdened with an unsuitable property for their business concerns. This was suffered at the time of the purchase of the building. On this analysis, the action was time-barred.

New Islington and Hackney Housing Association Ltd v Pollard Thomas and Edwards Ltd (2001)

(The facts of this case, and the position regarding limitation in respect of breach of contract, are set out at 7.2.1 above.)

The claimant also brought proceedings against the defendants in tort. However, the result was the same: such proceedings were time-barred. Dyson J held that the claimant's cause of action accrued, at the latest, at the time of practical completion, as the buildings suffered from a lack of adequate sound insulation (and therefore economic loss had been sustained) from the outset.

The grounds upon which Dyson J distinguished *London Congregational Union v Harriss* are important to note (at 41):

'In *Harriss*, the damaging consequences of the defective drains were not immediately effective, since the drains were capable of functioning properly as drains, and did so function, for 20 months. Accordingly, the physical damage was not suffered until those damaging consequences first occurred. In the present case, the sound insulation was inadequate from the date of handover. It was never capable of being fit for the purpose. In the language of "damaging consequences", those consequences were immediately effective. From the outset, the building suffered from lack of adequate sound insulation ... It is the building that suffers from the defect, and that is what is required to enable the owner to complete his cause of action in negligence.'

Tesco v Costain Construction Ltd (2004)

The defendant building contractors were engaged by the claimant to design and build a new superstore. Practical completion occurred in 1990, but the building was subsequently damaged by a catastrophic fire which broke out in 2001. The claimant alleged that the defendant was negligent and/or in breach of contract for failing to install appropriate fire-stopping measures.

The court held that the claimant's cause of action in tort accrued upon completion of the building; the store was less valuable from that moment onwards than it would have been had the fire-inhibiting measures been incorporated into it. In other words, given that a 'special relationship' was held to exist between the parties (by virtue of the underlying contract, if nothing else), the claimant suffered actionable damage in the form of 'pure economic loss' from the outset, and not from the date of the fire.

The judge distinguished *Pirelli* and *London Congregational Union v Harriss* (cases in which the cause of action was held to arise on the date of the physical damage, not completion of the works) on the basis that the nature of the deficiency in question was the 'lack of a desirable attribute' (i.e. more extensive fire-stopping) rendering the building less capable of resisting fire damage, as opposed to the use of unsuitable materials which made physical damage inevitable.

Abbott v Will Gannon & Smith Ltd (2005)

The defendants were structural engineers who were engaged in 1995 by the claimant hoteliers to carry out design work to remedy structural defects in a bay window at the claimant's hotel in Torquay. In March 1997, remedial works were completed pursuant to the defendants' designs. Two years later, in 1999, the bay window suffered further damage, necessitating further remedial works at a cost of £20,000. The claimant issued proceedings in both contract and tort in September 2003, although subsequently conceded that the claim in contract was time-barred.

The defendants sought to argue that the property was defective upon completion of the initial remedial works, the claimants suffered economic loss upon this date as the bay window was defective. The Court of Appeal rejected this argument and followed *Pirelli*. On this basis, any 'economic loss' was not in fact sustained by the claimant until 1999. This was the date when the defective design works manifested themselves in such a way that the value of the building was affected.

7.4.3 Summary

- In tort, limitation runs from the 'date of damage'.

- It is not always straightforward to establish when such 'damage' occurs.

- To be actionable, the damage complained of must be a 'measurable relevant loss'. Potential, or even inevitable, damage is not sufficient.

- What constitutes a 'measurable relevant loss' will depend heavily on the facts in every case:

  - The type of loss claimed will dictate when the 'relevant damage' occurs. Thus a cause of action may arise after physical damage manifests itself in the building.

  - In some circumstances, damage will be suffered from the outset. This will inevitably take the form of 'pure economic loss'.

  - In terms of physical damage, only in exceptional circumstances will a 'doomed from the start' scenario be established.

  - Following *Abbott v Gannon*, it may be the case that 'pure economic loss' is not actually suffered for the purposes of triggering limitation until the defect in question manifests itself so as to affect the value of the building.

  - Where the defect in question is flawed design or construction which renders physical damage inevitable (as opposed to a defect which is simply the lack of a 'desirable attribute' (such as sound insulation or fire stopping)), then it appears that limitation will run from when such physical damage occurs.

7.5 'DISCOVERABILITY' AND LATENT DAMAGE

There will be occasions when the law provides apparently unjust results, especially when a claimant is prevented from bringing a claim because damage to his property has occurred before he in fact became aware of it, or could have been reasonably expected to become aware of it.

Indeed, the potential injustice of *Pirelli* was recognised by Lord Scarman in the course of delivering his judgment in the same case:

'It must be … unjustifiable in principle that a cause of action should be held to accrue before it is possible to discover any injury or damage. A law which produces such a result … is harsh and absurd.'

7.5.1 Latent Damage Act 1986

Where damage resulting from an act of negligence is not discoverable until after it actually occurs, a claimant may be derive assistance from the provisions of the *Latent Damage Act* 1986 ('the LDA 1986') which operate so as to extend the limitation period in which to bring an action.

Essentially, the LDA 1986 inserted additional sections into the *Limitation Act* 1980 (specifically, ss. 14A, 14B and 32(5)). These apply to actions in negligence; they will not apply to a claim brought in contract (see *J K Buckingham v Iron Trades Mutual Insurance* (1990)).

7.5.1.1 Extension of limitation period

Limitation Act 1980, ss. 14A, 14B

'14A Special time limit for negligence actions where facts relevant to cause of action are not known at date of accrual

(1) This section applies to any action for damages for negligence, other than one to which section 11 of this Act applies [personal injury], where the starting date for reckoning the period of limitation under subsection 4(b) below falls after the date on which the cause of action accrued.

(2) Section 2 of this Act shall not apply to an action to which this section applies.

(3) An action to which this section applies shall not be brought after the expiration of the period applicable in accordance with subsection (4) below.

(4) That period is either:

(a) six years from the date on which the cause of action accrued; or

(b) three years from the starting date as defined by subsection (5) below, if that period expires later than the period mentioned in paragraph (a) above.

(5) For the purposes of this section, the starting date for reckoning the period of limitation under subsection (4)(b) above is the earliest date on which the plaintiff or any person in whom the cause of action was vested before him first had both the knowledge required for bringing an action for damages in respect of the relevant damage and a right to bring such an action.

(6) In subsection (5) above "the knowledge required for bringing an action for damages in respect of the relevant damage" means knowledge both:

(a) of the material facts about the damage in respect of which damages are claimed; and

(b) of the other facts relevant to the current action mentioned in subsection (8) below.

(7) For the purposes of subsection (6)(a) above, the material facts about the damage are such facts about the damage as would lead a reasonable person who had suffered such damage to consider it sufficiently serious to justify his instituting proceedings for damages against a defendant who did not dispute liability and was able to satisfy a judgment.

(8) The other facts referred to in subsection (6)(b) above are:

(a) that the damage was attributable in whole or in part to the act or omission which is alleged to constitute negligence; and

(b) the identity of the defendant; and

(c) if it is alleged that the act or omission was that of a person other than the defendant, the identity of that person and the additional facts supporting the bringing of an action against the defendant.

(9) Knowledge that any acts or omissions did or did not, as a matter of law, involve negligence is irrelevant for the purposes of subsection (5) above.

(10) For the purposes of this section a person's knowledge includes knowledge which he might reasonably have been expected to acquire:

(a) from facts observable or ascertainable by him; or

(b) from facts ascertainable by him with the help of appropriate expert advice which it is reasonable for him to seek;

but a person shall not be taken by virtue of this subsection to have knowledge of a fact ascertainable only with the help of expert evidence so long as he has taken all reasonable steps to obtain (and, where appropriate, to act on) that advice.

14B Overriding time limit for negligence actions not involving personal injuries

(1) An action for damages for negligence, other than one to which section 11 of this Act applies, shall not be brought after the expiration of fifteen years from this date (or, if more than one, from the last of the dates) on which there occurred any act or omission:

(a) which is alleged to constitute negligence; and

(b) to which the damage in respect of which damages are claimed is alleged to be attributable (in whole or in part).

(2) This section barred the right of action in a case to which subsection (1) above applies notwithstanding that:

(a) the cause of action has not yet accrued; or

(b) where section 14A of this Act applies to the action, the date which is for the purposes of that section the starting date for reckoning the period mentioned in subsection (4)(b) of that section has not yet occurred;

before the end of the period of limitation prescribed by this section.'

Summary

- A party's cause of action in negligence will still accrue when damage occurs.
- Pursuant to *Limitation Act* 1980, s. 14A the limitation period for bringing an action in negligence will expire after either six years from when the cause of action accrues

(i.e. from the date of the damage itself) or three years from the 'starting date' (often referred to as the 'date of discoverability' of the damage), whichever is later.

- Pursuant to *Limitation Act* 1980, s. 14A(5) the 'starting date' is the earliest date on which the would-be claimant had both the knowledge required for bringing an action for damages in respect of the relevant damage and a right to bring such an action.

- Pursuant to *Limitation Act* 1980, s. 14B in all cases, the limitation period for bringing an action in negligence will expire 15 years after the date of the negligent act.

- The position is different where defects have been concealed is subject to different rules (as to which, see 7.6.1 below).

7.5.1.2   One limitation period, not two

Busby v Cooper (1996)

In 1986, the claimant purchased a house which was the subject of a mining report prepared by the first defendant. In 1994, the claimant sought to add another party as the third defendant to the proceedings on the grounds that he had negligently advised Abbey National (the second defendant) that the mining report was suitable for lending purposes. It was common ground that such a joinder was outside of the primary limitation period, but the claimant argued that she did not have the requisite knowledge for the purposes of *Limitation Act* 1980, s. 14A until 1991. The third defendant sought to argue that the two separate subparagraphs stipulate two separate limitation periods.

The Court of Appeal, in rejecting the third defendant's submissions, held that the effect of *Limitation Act* 1980, s. 14A was not to impose two separate limitation periods; rather it is to be viewed as a device to extend the primary limitation period in applicable circumstances. The action was not statute-barred.

7.5.1.3 'Relevant knowledge'

Halford v Brookes (1991)

In this case, the subject matter of which concerned a civil action against two men who had been charged with the murder of the plaintiff's daughter, Lord Donaldson MR held that 'relevant knowledge' for the purposes of extending the primary time limit meant 'reasonable belief'. Mere suspicion that another party was responsible for the relevant damage, especially if unsubstantiated, is not enough.

Spencer-Ward v Humberts (1995)

The courts have encouraged a commonsensical approach to what constitutes 'relevant knowledge', taking into account the object of the statute and the injustice that it was intended to mitigate. The court considered that:

> 'There is a danger of being too clever and it would usually be possible to find some fact of which a plaintiff did not become sure until later. It would be a pity if a desire to be indulgent to plaintiffs led the court to be unfair to defendants.'

Mortgage Corporation v Lambert & Co and Another (2000)

These proceedings concerned a negligent valuation of a property by a surveyor. The Court of Appeal ruled that 'knowledge' for the purposes of *Limitation Act* 1980, s. 14A (i.e. knowledge that damage has been suffered which was sufficiently serious so as to justify issuing proceedings) does not mean that a claimant will know enough to be in a position to quantify precisely his loss. Rather, he must be aware that the damage is sufficiently serious to justify bringing an action.

New Islington and Hackney Housing Association Ltd v Pollard Thomas and Edwards Ltd (2001)

(The facts of this case are set out at 7.2.1 above.) The claimant housing association, in order to get around difficulties with limitation, attempted to argue that it did not have the 'relevant knowledge' in respect of the defects until after 1 May 1995 (which was the 'cut-off' date for limitation purposes). Dyson J ruled that as solicitors for the claimant housing association had a 'strong indication' that there was a design problem and that the architect was responsible in early 1995, the action was statute-barred.

7.6 SUCCESSIVE OWNERS

Latent Damage Act 1986, s. 3

'3(1) Subject to the following provisions of this section, where:

(a) a cause of action ("the original cause of action") has accrued to any person in respect of any negligence to which damage to any property in which he has an interest is attributable (in whole or in part); and

(b) another person acquires an interest in that property after the date on which the original cause of action accrued but before the material facts about the damage have become known to any person who, at the time when he first has knowledge of those facts, has any interest in the property;

a fresh cause of action in respect of that negligence shall accrue to that other person on the date on which he acquires his interest in the property.

(2) A cause of action accruing to any person by virtue of subsection (1) above:

(a) shall be treated as if based on breach of a duty of care at common law owed to the person to whom it accrues; and

(b) shall be treated for the purposes of section 14A of the 1980 Act ... as having accrued on the date on which the original cause of action accrued.'

If the above conditions are satisfied, the effect of *Latent Damage Act* 1986, s. 3 is that in circumstances where a person acquires an interest in property, a fresh cause of action negligence in respect of damage to that property will accrue to that person against a party who caused the damage.

However, the cause of action will accrue on the date upon which the cause of action accrued to the *original* owner of the property (and not start afresh every time a proprietary interest in the property passes hands).

Should the new owner obtain the relevant 'knowledge' in respect of the latent damage at a later date than the original owner, then time may be extended.

7.6.1 Concealment, mistake and fraud

Limitation Act 1980, s. 32

'32 Postponement of limitation period in case of fraud, concealment or mistake

(1) Subject to [subsections (3) and (4A)] below, where in the case of any action for which a period of limitation is prescribed by this Act, either:

(a) the action is based upon the fraud of the defendant; or

(b) any fact relevant to the plaintiff's right of action has been deliberately concealed from him by the defendant; or

(c) the action is for relief from the consequences of a mistake;

the period of limitation shall not begin to run until the plaintiff has discovered the fraud, concealment or mistake (as the case may be) or could with reasonable diligence have discovered it.

References in this subsection to the defendant include references to the defendant's agent and to any person through whom the defendant claims and his agent.

(2) For the purposes of subsection (1) above, deliberate commission of a breach of duty in circumstances in which it is unlikely to be discovered for some time amounts to a deliberate concealment of the facts involved in that breach of duty.

(3) Nothing in this section shall enable any action:

(a) to recover, or recover the value of, any property; or

(b) to enforce any charge against, or set aside any transaction affecting, any property;

to be brought against the purchaser of the property or any person claiming through him in any case where the property has been purchased for valuable consideration by an innocent third party since the fraud or concealment or (as the case may be) the transaction in which the mistake was made took place.

(4) A purchaser is an innocent third party for the purposes of this section:

(a) in the case of fraud or concealment of any fact relevant to the plaintiff's right of action, if he was not a party to the fraud or (as the case may be) to the concealment of that fact and did not at the time of the purchase know or have reason to believe that the fraud or concealment had taken place; and

(b) in the case of mistake, if he did not at the time of the purchase know or have reason to believe that the mistake had been made.

...

(5) Sections 14A and 14B of this Act shall not apply to any action to which subsection (1)(b) above applies (and accordingly the period of limitation referred to in that subsection, in any case to which either of those sections would otherwise apply, is the period applicable under section 2 of this Act).'

The practical application of *Limitation Act* 1980, s. 32 in the context of building disputes normally arises in circumstances where the defect in question that has caused damage has been deliberately concealed, such concealment constituting fraud for the purposes of the Act.

Should this occur, a party may bring an action against another party within six years from the earliest date when the concealment was discovered or was reasonably discoverable.

This is the position in both claims brought in contract and in negligence (i.e. in respect of the latter, the 15-year longstop provision will not apply).

Clark v Woor (1965)

The defendant was a builder who, in 1953, deliberately entered into the contract knowing that he could not perform it in accordance with its terms, which were to construct a house with Dorking bricks. The defendant was aware that there was a delay in obtaining Dorking bricks so, without telling the claimant, he substituted the required Dorking bricks with Ockley bricks.

The claimant noticed that some of the bricks were beginning to flake in 1961. Following an architect's inspection, it turned out that around one-quarter of the bricks used were rejects or seconds. A cement rendering to the outside of the property would be required to prevent further damage.

The court held that the defendant was aware that the claimant was relying upon him to perform his contract and to treat the claimant in a 'decent, honest way'. In the absence of any supervision of the works, the claimant was dependent upon the defendant for the 'honest performance of the contract'.

The court ruled that in the circumstances, the claimant had proved that the right of action was concealed by fraud and that claim was not statute-barred.

Although the claimant had not discovered the damage until some eight years after the breach of contract, he had made enquiries as soon as the flaking was noticed. The court considered what kind of conduct was required by a claimant to take advantage of (what was then) *Limitation Act* 1939, s. 26(b) (at 654):

> '... I am also satisfied ... that the ordinary man and woman who asked a builder to build a house for them could not be expected to know the difference between a Dorking brick and an Ockley brick, and unless they were actually on the site and had knowledge of brickwork even less could they know the difference between a good Ockley brick and a bad Ockley brick. It follows, it seems to me, that in no sense could the plaintiffs be held to have done anything else than use reasonable diligence'.

The damages were assessed as being the cost of the necessary remedial works had the same been carried out in 1961, the date upon which the claimant discovered his right of action.

Applegate v Moss (1971)

The defendant was a builder who entered into a contract with the claimants for the construction of two houses on concrete raft foundations for the price of £1,900. It was a term of the contract that the foundations were to be carried out in a substantial and workmanlike manner. Works began in 1957 and the claimants occupied the premises later that year. In 1966 the premises were evacuated when a survey undertaken on behalf of the claimants indicated that the foundations were so defective that the properties were not fit for habitation. At the time of the evacuation, the properties were worth £2,900, and the claimants issued proceedings to recover their loss. The defendant argued that the proceedings were time-barred.

The Court of Appeal held that in circumstances where the defendant had covered up his 'disgraceful work', the claimants had no opportunity of inspecting the same and the defendant 'knew all of the facts', the defendant will not be entitled to rely on the *Limitation Act* as a defence to a claim.

To be 'fraudulent' for the purposes of the Act does not require any 'moral turpitude'; rather, the conduct of the builder must be shown to be unconscionable. Instead:

'The section applies whenever the conduct of the defendant or his agent has been such as to hide from the plaintiff the existence of his right of action, in such circumstances that it would be inequitable to allow the defendant to rely on the lapse of time as a bar to the claim.'

King v Victor Parsons & Co (1973)

The defendants were estate developers who agreed to construct a semi-detached property for the claimant in 1961. Prior to construction, the defendants took architectural advice and were informed that the site was, up until 1954, used as a rubbish tip. As a result, the architect advised that either reinforced concrete raft foundations or piled foundations connected by reinforced concrete ground beams be dug. The defendants chose to ignore this advice, and construction of the property began without piled or raft foundations. Instead, the builder simply laid down spreading concrete reinforced with a 'makeshift' grillage as an underlay for the floors. In 1968 the claimant was woken at night by a loud crack. Further cracking occurred and subsequent surveys established that the property was uninhabitable and would have to be pulled down. The claimant sued the defendants for damages in 1969.

In holding that the *Limitation Act* did not apply so as to bar the claimant's claim, the Court of Appeal ruled that in order to establish 'fraud' it was not necessary to show that a party took active steps to conceal his wrongdoing. Rather, it was enough that such wrongdoing was either knowingly done (with nothing said to the other) or recklessly done (like the 'man who turns a blind eye') to conceal the other party's right of action.

However, if on the facts a defendant merely commits an 'honest blunder' then he can avail himself of the statute. It seems that some affectation of conscience is therefore necessary in order to prove deliberate concealment: merely pleading that the defendant 'ought to have known' of his errors is not enough.

London Borough of Lewisham v Leslie (1980)

The claimant was the successor to the London County Council which had engaged the defendant contractors to construct four tower blocks in Lewisham in 1960. Construction works were completed in 1961. During the course of a routine fire inspection in 1971, it was discovered that there was a gap between the concrete shell and the cladding of one of the buildings. Further investigations were carried out and it transpired that the contractor had neglected to fit approximately of the required number of ties to seal the cladding to the concrete shell. Considerable remedial works were required and an action was brought in 1976 against the defendant to recover the costs of the same. The defendant argued that the proceedings were time-barred.

The court found that the defects had been kept concealed both from itself and its predecessors; accordingly, time did not run against its claim until discovery of the defects in 1971.

The court considered that no distinction should be drawn between small-scale residential works and large, publicly-funded tower blocks: the mere fact that London County Council employed architects and surveyors who may have been in a position to notice any defects as they arose was not automatically sufficient for the defendant to defeat the allegation of deliberate concealment. This will be a matter of fact in each case. As Lord Denning MR explained (at 28):

'It only requires a little imagination to think of circumstances in which workmen may do their work badly, leaving defects – which the architect or supervisor would not discover, even by using reasonable diligence … It is all very well to talk about the Council having its own architects and supervisors. But these gentlemen may have been misled by the contractors. The bad work may have been done when they were away or their backs were turned for some good reason.'

Peco Arts Inc v Hazlitt Gallery (1983)

The defendants were well-known and highly-regarded art dealers from whom the claimant purchased a painting, which was alleged to be by a famous nineteenth-century French artist, in 1970. The claimant did not seek an independent inspection until 1976, when the painting was valued for insurance purposes. In 1981 the painting was valued for a second time, when it was discovered to be a fake. Proceedings were brought against the defendants for the recovery of the purchase price as money paid under a mistake of fact.

The court held that the claimant's claim was not time-barred. Despite not obtaining an independent valuation and/or inspection at the time of purchase, the claimant had used 'reasonable diligence' to ensure the authenticity of the painting: in addition to the claimant seeking an inspection in 1976, it was reasonable in all the circumstances to rely on the defendants' reputation as experts; hence *Limitation Act* 1980, s. 32(1)(c) applied.

William Hill v Sunley (1983)

These proceedings concerned defective cladding to a building constructed by the defendant contractor between 1960 and 1961. The cladding was fitted by a specialist subcontractor. It became apparent in late 1971 that the cladding was defective, although it was not until 1974 that positive signs of movement were noticed. Proceedings were issued against the defendant in 1975.

The Court of Appeal held that the claimant's action was time-barred. It was not enough for the purposes of establishing fraudulent or deliberate concealment simply to show that the defendant had carried out shoddy work and 'covered it up' with later building works. To do so, a claimant must prove that the conscience of the contractor (or subcontractor) was so affected that it was, in all the circumstances, unconscionable for him to have proceeded with the works without putting the defective work right. Further, a claimant will struggle to prove that defects are concealed if the same would have been obvious to a party charged with supervising or signing off the works.

Kaliszewska v John Clague & Partners (1984)

The claimant engaged the defendant architect to design a single-storey dwelling-house at a Kaliszewska site in Kent. The ground was largely composed of London clay. Unbeknown to the claimant, the defendant's design was defective in that it did not make proper provisions for settlement and heave conditions which should have been anticipated on the site. In 1974, four years after the house was completed, cracking appeared. The cracks worsened in 1976 and in 1978 an independent expert advised that underpinning was necessary. The claimant brought an action to recover the costs of remedial works in 1982.

The judge ruled that the property was an 'exceptional' case and was satisfied that the building was 'doomed from the start' (see 7.4.2 above), with some movement damage having in fact occurred at a very early stage (in 1971). The judge further held that the defendant was guilty only of incompetence, and not deliberate concealment, even though the designer had deliberately rejected contemporaneous architectural wisdom as 'idealistic'.

Kijowski v New Capital Properties (1987)

The defendants were responsible for the construction of a house in 1971 that was purchased by the claimant in 1978. In 1981, as a result of differential settlement underneath the house, a large crack appeared. By 1982, the damage had become so extensive that the house was deemed unsaleable. It was found that during the course of construction, the defendants had (amongst other things) ignored approved plans in respect of joists at roof and first-floor level, and laid defective foundations. The claimant began an action against the defendants in 1984.

The court held that the proceedings were not statute-barred, as the damage complained of (i.e. the cracking) manifested itself well within the primary (i.e. six-year) limitation period. However, the judge went on to rule that, in any event, the defendants had deliberately concealed facts relevant to the claimant's cause of action which would have otherwise postponed the start of the limitation period. The court considered that that to avail himself of *Limitation Act* 1980, s. 32, a claimant must show that the builder has

> '… knowingly done bad work which has been covered up so that bad work is not likely to be detected by a purchaser or his successors'.

The defendants sought to reduce the damages awarded to the claimant on the grounds that the claimant was contributorily negligent for not obtaining a survey prior to purchasing the house. The court refused to entertain this submission, holding that given the fact that the house was relatively new and free from any defects which would be obvious to a non-expert, the claimant's decision to proceed without a survey was reasonable; consequently the award of damages would not be reduced.

[For an example of a case in which the court ruled that a claimant may be contributorily negligent in not obtaining a survey prior to purchase, see *Perry v Tendring DC* (1984).]

E Clarke & Sons (Coaches) Ltd v Axtell Yates (1989)

In 1977 the claimant engaged the second defendants, a firm of building contractors, to construct a garage and adjoining car park. The works were certified as being finally complete in March 1980. In 1983 the claimant discovered water leaking into an inspection pit in the garage and more extensive checks revealed that there were numerous defects with the building. Proceedings were not issued until October 1986. On the facts, whilst the claimant was able to prove bad workmanship, he was unable to establish deliberate concealment of the same. In other words, it is not enough for a claimant to show that a relevant fact has been concealed; only a deliberate concealment of a relevant fact will suffice for the purposes of *Limitation Act* 1980, s. 32.

Gray v T P Bennett & Son (1989)

The claimant brought proceedings in 1983 in respect of defective construction works which were carried out in or around 1962 by the fourth defendants, who were responsible for erecting a blockwork fascia to a building, to be tied to the concrete shell by wall ties and reinforced concrete projections (or 'nibs'). Completion of the works was carried out in 1963 with final completion two years later.

When the blockwork fascia began to bow in 1979, investigations revealed that a large proportion of the 'nibs' had been hacked back to overcome problems with alignment, leaving the blockwork in a perilous condition. Proceedings were issued in 1983.

The court held that the fourth defendants had deliberately concealed the 'butchering of the concrete nibs' and that the action was not statute-barred; the hacking was not reasonably discoverable until 1979. Further, the court rejected the argument that the first defendant, a firm of architects, should have discovered the hacking upon a reasonable inspection of the works. In the circumstances, it was not the architect's duty to inspect the alignment of the panels.

British Steel plc v Wyvern Structures Ltd (1996)

This was a claim in respect of defective bellows units designed and manufactured by the defendants and installed at the claimant's power station in 1978. An explosion occurred in 1990 which resulted from a rupture in one of the bellows units. The claimant alleged that the damage resulted from failure of a single hinge-to-flange weld during the fit-up and plate-cutting process of the bellows, and that the presence of excessive weld was a 'fair indication that those in charge of this fabrication ... were aware that all was not well with the fit-up'.

The court refused to find that deliberate concealment of the weld had taken place. Whilst it was possible that an oversized weld resulting from defective workmanship could have 'slipped through', it does not follow that the same was deliberately concealed. Errors in the welding process were more likely to result from boredom or neglect, rather than a conscious attempt to patch over bad work.

Sheldon & others v RHM Outhwaite Ltd (1996)

In 1992, the claimants (all of whom were Lloyd's Names) brought proceedings against the defendants for negligence, breach of contract and breach of fiduciary duty.

The defendants contested that their actions were time-barred, such breaches having occurred in or around 1982. The claimants responded by contending that relevant facts to their causes of action had been deliberately concealed by the defendants in 1984 and, accordingly, limitation did not expire until six years following the discovery of such concealment.

The House of Lords held that *Limitation Act* 1980, s. 32(1)(b) applied in circumstances where a deliberate concealment of relevant facts took place after the accrual of a cause of action. Lord Browne-Wilkinson, in delivering the leading judgment, explained that any other construction of the Act

'... would lead to an unfair result inconsistent with the underlying rationale of the section, viz. that the defendants would be entitled to benefit from their own unconscionable behaviour by deliberately concealing the facts relevant to the plaintiffs' cause of action'.

Cave v Robinson Jarvis & Rolf (2003)

The defendants were a firm of solicitors who, in March 1989, acted on behalf of the claimant to obtain mooring rights for 100 years over land in the Isle of Wight which belonged to a third party company. In 1994, receivers of the company's bank informed the claimant that his mooring rights were no longer exercisable. In March 1996, the District Land Registry informed the claimant that his mooring rights were not entered on the Land Register. The claimant issued proceedings against the defendants in January 1998.

The House of Lords held that the claimant's action was statute-barred. Where a defendant is unaware of an error or of a failure to take reasonable care, then such conduct cannot be brought within *Limitation Act*, s. 32(2) so as to prevent time from running until the discovery of the same.

However, if a party inadvertently acts in breach of contract or duty but later realises that he has done so and fails to inform the party who may be affected by such a breach, then that party is likely to be able to prove that such an error has been deliberately or recklessly concealed from him and rely on *Limitation Act*, s. 32 if the primary limitation period has already expired.

7.6.2 Summary

- The basic principle is that a claim must be brought within the statutory period.

- The position is different where facts relevant to a claimant's cause of action are concealed by the defendant. In such circumstances, time will not run until the claimant discovers the concealment or should with reasonable diligence have discovered it.

- For the purposes of *Limitation Act* 1980, s. 14A one must look at the information available to the claimant at the relevant time and establish what a reasonable person would have drawn from that information.

- If the works are supervised by a different party then this may have an effect on whether defects can be said to be 'concealed'. This is a question of fact.

8
Defects and the project team

8.1 INTRODUCTION: SCOPE OF THE PROFESSIONAL DUTY OF CARE

Modern-day construction work often involves a complicated matrix of relationships between professionals. Although largely regulated by contract, it is now settled law that a construction professional will owe a concurrent duty of care that is co-extensive with his contractual obligations.

Given the fact that construction projects often take many months or even years to complete, members of a project team are frequently engaged for longer periods than in other industries. In this respect, the very nature of the building industry has distinctly coloured the development of the construction professional's duty of care.

8.2 ONGOING DUTY OF REVIEW

An architect or structural engineer will often have a duty to revisit or review services which he has provided at an earlier stage:

London Borough of Merton v Lowe (1981)

The Court of Appeal upheld the decision of Stabb J at first instance who held that an architect was under a 'continuing duty of design'. The subsequent discovery of a defect in the design, initially and justifiably thought to have been suitable, reactivates or revives the architect's duty in relation to design and imposes upon them the duty to take such steps as are necessary to correct the results of that initially defective design.

Chelmsford District Council v T J Evers (1984)

In this case, an engineer was held to be under a duty to review his design 'as necessary' in the absence of any contractual provisions to the contrary.

J Sainsbury plc v Broadway Malyan (1998)

The duty of constant review should not be construed too widely: in this case, the court held that it only comes into play as and when the occasion arises to look at or review the design (for example, if there is a possibility of a design deficiency or a need for the design to be modified).

Department of National Heritage v Steensen Varming Mulcahy (1998)

Construction professionals are expected to be proactive. In this particular case, it was not open to a mechanical engineer to defend an allegation of negligent design by claiming that his design was prepared with proper skill and care at the outset but was subsequently rendered inappropriate as a result of factors out of his control.

Gloucestershire Health Authority v MA Torpy & Partners (1997)

There may be occasions where clients pay more for architects, engineers or quantity surveyors of an especially high standard. A distinction may be drawn between 'specialist' engineers and 'general practice' engineers. In such cases, the duty owed by these professionals may be more onerous than the conventional standard of the ordinary competent and skilled practitioner.

8.3 FITNESS FOR PURPOSE

Whilst the question of whether a construction professional has impliedly warranted that a particular structure is fit for purpose is ultimately a question of fact, in the absence of any specific facts the construction professional will not normally be subject to such an obligation.

IBA v EMI and BICC (1980)

Whilst not deciding the point, the House of Lords considered that there was no obstruction in principle to the imposition of an implied warranty that an architect's or engineer's design will be fit for its ultimate purpose.

George Hawkins v Chrysler (UK) Ltd (1986)

Despite the ruling in *IBA v EMI and BICC* (above), the courts will be reluctant to sanction a blanket extension to the scope of a professional's duty of care to encompass fitness for purpose; the court must look to the particular facts of each case to see whether there is a basis for grounding such a warranty.

Payne v Setchell (2002)

In the absence of 'special circumstances', a construction professional will not normally be taken to have warranted that a particular structure is fit for purpose.

8.4 LIMITATION OF LIABILITY CLAUSES

A limitation clause is one that limits a professional's liability without attempting to exclude such liability altogether. If there is a contract between the parties, and the performing party is negligent, then the extent of his liability may be regulated by a limitation clause in the contract itself.

William Hill v Bernard Sunley (1983)

Where a professional's contract provides that damages from any breach of contract will be limited (in time or extent), then his duty of care will be limited only to avoid causing the damage for which he has accepted liability under the contract, and no more.

BHP Petroleum Ltd v British Steel plc (2000)

Limitation clauses may attract a less stringent judicial approach than exclusion clauses, but the more extreme the effects of a limitation clause, the more stringent the approach will become. They must be clearly expressed in order to bite, and in the case of any ambiguity, the clause will generally be given the meaning which is the least onerous of the potential constructions.

8.5 NET CONTRIBUTION CLAUSES

The rules of causation in negligence may have potentially very onerous repercussions for the construction professional. Consider, for example, the position of an architect on a building project that goes wrong, resulting in substantial loss to the employer. The loss incurred may well be the fault of many parties, but say for argument's sake that the architect is 25 per cent to blame and the remainder of the responsibility lies with negligent building subcontractors.

The architect, however, could be sued by the employer and will be liable for *all* the damages, whatever his 'fair' share of the blame. In theory, the architect may make a claim for contribution from the subcontractors under the *Civil Liability (Contribution) Act* 1978, but this does not provide much comfort if the said building contractor is insolvent.

Because of these risks, construction professionals are now likely to include 'net contribution clauses' in their standard terms and conditions. Such clauses attempt to limit a professional's liability to the claimant to his 'fair share' of the damages, where the claimant's loss has been caused by more than one of its advisors.

RIBA Standard Form of Agreement for the Appointment of an Architect (SFA/99)

'7.3 In any action or proceedings brought against the Architect under or in connection with the Agreement whether in contract, negligence, tort or howsoever the Architect's liability for loss or damage in respect of any one occurrence of series of occurrences arising out of one event shall be limited to whichever is the lesser of the sum:

7.3.1 stated in the Appendix; or

7.3.2 such sum as it is just and equitable for the Architect to pay having regard to the extent of his responsibility for the loss and/or damage in question when compared with the responsibilities of contractors, subcontractors, consultants and other persons for that loss and/or damage. Such sum to be assessed on the basis that such persons are deemed to have provided contractual undertakings to the Client no less onerous than those of the Architect under the Agreement and had paid to the Client such sums as it would be just and equitable for them to pay having regard to the extent of their responsibility for that loss and/or damage.'

Clause 7.3 from the Standard Form of Agreement for the Appointment of an Architect (SFA/1999) is reproduced here with permission from RIBA Enterprises.

9
Remedies

9.1 DEFECTIVE WORK: THE BASIC PRINCIPLE

In an action for breach of contract, damages are awarded on the principle that the claimant is to be put, so far as is possible by monetary award, in the position he would have been in if the contractual duties had properly been carried out. In an action for negligence, the claimant is to be put in the position he would have been had the tortfeasor not been negligent.

Under defects liability clauses (considered in Chapter 2 above) the contract will provide for specific remedies given certain circumstances. However, unless clear words are used, the defects liability provisions will not prevent a simple action for breach of contract or negligence arising out of the existence of a defect.

One way of assessing, in monetary terms, a loss caused by defective work is to consider the cost of rectifying the defect. A different way of assessing the loss is by reference to the reduced value of the final product in light of the existing defect. It is sometimes claimed that even after repair works, there remains a residual diminution in value. If right, these circumstances may justify a combination of both approaches in assessing the true measure of loss.

9.2 COST OF REINSTATEMENT

In the case of a defect in building, the normal measure of loss is the cost of reinstatement.

Thornton v Place (1832)

In a contract to slate a house, the builder brought an action for the contract price. The owner was allowed to set up a reduction in the price of the damages he had sustained through the builder's defective work. The measure of the deduction was the sum which it would take to alter the work, so as to make it comply with the specification.

Dakin v Lee (1916)

Approving the judgment in *Thornton v Place*, the Court of Appeal stated that an owner, sued for the price of the work, was entitled to deduct such an amount as was sufficient to put that insufficiently done work into the condition in which it out to have been according to the contract.

Hoenig v Isaacs (1952)

The claimant sued for the price of his work consisting of the decoration and furnishing of the defendant's flat. The defendant sought to avoid payment of the balance owing (some 40 per cent of the contract price) on account of defects in the furniture which nevertheless he was using. The court held that the contract had been substantially performed so that the claimant was entitled to the balance, less the cost of making good such defects as the defendant was able to prove.

East Ham Corp v Bernard Sunley (1966)

After the completion of the construction of a school and some two years after the architect had given his final certificate, stone panels fixed to the exterior walls fell off owing to defective fixing by the contractors and were repaired by the local authority, who sought to recover the cost from the contractors in an arbitration. The proper measure of damages was the cost of the reinstatement.

Radford v De Froberville (1977)

The claimant obtained planning permission to build a house on a plot of land forming part of the grounds of his existing house. The claimant sold the plot to the defendant on terms that she would build the proposed house, and that she would erect a wall to specification on the plot bought so as to divide it from the claimant's land and to maintain it in good repair. No such wall was built. The court held that the correct measure of damages was the cost to the claimant of erecting a wall to the contract specification on his own land and not the amount by which the claimant's land as an investment property was diminished by the absence of the wall.

9.3 WHERE COST OF REINSTATEMENT IS INAPPROPRIATE

Diminution in value may be appropriate where the defect is irreparable, or where the cost of reinstatement is out of all proportion with the benefit gained.

Applegate v Moss (1971)

In 1957, the defendant built two houses for the claimant in accordance with plans and specifications which provided for concrete raft foundations and a concrete mix of a specified quality. The price was £1,900. Upon attempting to sell one of the properties in 1965 it was revealed that the foundations were so defective that the houses were unsaleable, unsafe to live in and irreparable. The court held that the claimant's loss was therefore the whole market value the claimant would have had in 1965 if the houses had been properly built, namely, £2,900.

Darlington Borough Council v Wiltshier Northern Ltd (1995)

The Court of Appeal confirmed that in the case of a building contract, the usual rule is cost of cure, i.e., the cost of remedying the defect. However, where the cost of remedying the defects involves expense out of all proportion to the benefit which could accrue from it, the court is entitled to adopt the alternative measure of difference of the value of the works.

Ruxley Electronics and Construction Ltd v Forsyth (1996)

In a contract to build a swimming pool, the specification stated that the pool should have a diving area of seven-and-a-half feet. On completion, the depth was only six feet nine inches, although this was not unsafe for diving. The test of reasonableness plays a central part in determining the basis of recovery. The cost of reinstatement (effectively rebuilding the pool) was held by the House of Lords to be unreasonable given that it would be out of all proportion with the benefit to be obtained. There was no diminution in value and no damages under this head were recoverable.

G W Atkins v Scott (1991)

The claimant company sued for the price of work done in the amount of £1,001.21. The defendant counterclaimed for defects in the tiling work, the cost of reinstatement of which was put somewhere between £500 and £1,200. The court considered that the defects were not of a serious nature. Diminution in value was more appropriate when the proportion of defective work was small in relation to the whole property and where the defect only affected the 'amenity value' of the property. There was no reason why the test for using a basis other than cost of reinstatement should not be the lack of reasonableness of the cost of that reinstatement.

Freeman v Niroomand (1996)

The claimant built a defective porch for the defendant, in that it should have had a cavity wall. The court awarded neither diminution in value (there was none) nor cost of cure (around £1,500) which was out of all proportion to the loss suffered and which money the householder would not have used to pull down the existing porch to build one strictly in accordance with the contractual specifications; £130 for loss of amenity was awarded.

9.4 WHERE DIMINUTION IN VALUE EXCEEDS COST OF REPAIR

Murphy v Brentwood DC (1991)

The Court of Appeal stated that the general principle of law was that the right to recover the diminution in loss of value on resale, caused by the defects in the foundation, would be limited in an amount which did not exceed the cost of repair. This was not disapproved by the House of Lords decision which overturned the Court of Appeal.

Newton Abbot Development Co Ltd v Stockman Bros (1931)

The claimants, as developers, had contracted with the defendants as contractors for the construction of a number of houses. After completion of the works, the claimants had sold the houses to individual purchasers at a profit. Thereafter defects due to faulty construction by the defendants appeared in the houses. The claimants, although under no legal liability to do so, had remedied these defects. They were held entitled to recover from the defendants the difference between the value of the houses as they ought to have been completed and their actual value as in fact completed, not the cost of effecting the remedial work.

9.5 THE RELEVANCE OF AN INTENTION TO EFFECT REPAIRS, AND WHO PAYS FOR THEM

Whether a party intends to effect repairs may be relevant, but not necessarily determinative, to whether cost of repair or diminution in value is the appropriate basis of recovery.

The fact that repairs have been paid for by someone other than the claimant is irrelevant.

C R Taylor (Wholesale) Ltd v Hepworths Ltd (1977)

The claimant owned a disused billiard hall which was destroyed by a fire for which the defendant was responsible. The property was in an area of potential redevelopment. The claimant's claim for the cost of reinstating the billiard hall – which would have amounted to more than £28,000 – failed because they had continued to own the property for its potential development value and had no intention of using it as a billiard hall. In these circumstances, the measure of damages was the diminution in its market value. Against this was set off the savings achieved in no longer having to clear the site for redevelopment. It was irrelevant that the claimant had been paid the theoretical cost of reinstating their premises by their insurers under the terms of the contract of insurance.

Dean v Ainley (1987)

The vendor of a house was in breach of his covenant to carry out certain works to prevent leakage from the patio into the cellar. The evidence was that, if the works had been carried out, dampness would not have been cured but would have been improved. This was enough to recover as damages the cost of the works which the vendor had undertaken to carry out. The court stated that the claimant did not have to go further by anything in the nature of an undertaking that he would in fact use any damages which he may recover in order to improve the cellar. The court expressly released the claimant from an undertaking to this effect which he had given voluntarily at the trial. It would have made no difference if he had said that he intended to sell the property or that it was uncertain whether he would do so or not. Nor would it make any difference if, having recovered £7,500, the claimant were to change his mind and decide – for whatever reason – not to spend anything on the improvement of the cellar.

Culworth Estates v Society of Licensed Victuallers (1991)

Leased premises were in a state of disrepair owing to breach by the tenant of the repairing covenants. The court held that it did not follow from the fact that the landlords did not themselves intend to carry out repairs that they were entitled only to nominal damages for the breach.

Linden Gardens Trust Ltd v Lenesta Sludge Disposals Ltd (1994)

Although there was no argument on the point in the House of Lords, Lord Griffiths observed in his judgment that the court will of course wish to be satisfied that the repairs have been or are likely to be carried out, but if they are carried out the cost of doing them must fall upon the defendant who broke his contract.

Darlington Borough Council v Wiltshier Northern Ltd (1995)

Lord Justice Steyn stated that in the field of building contracts, like sale of goods, it is no concern of the law what the claimant proposes to do with his damages. It is no precondition to the recovery of substantial damages that the claimant proposes to undertake the necessary repairs. English law adopts an objective approach to the ascertainment of damages for breach of contract.

Ruxley Electronics and Construction Ltd v Forsyth (1996)

(The facts of this case are set out at 9.3 above.) The finding of fact that the claimant's intention to rebuild the swimming pool would not persist for long after the conclusion of the litigation was relevant to the reasonableness of the basis of assessment to be made.

G W Atkins v Scott (1991)

(The facts of this case are set out at 9.3 above.) It was held that the desire of the building owner to effect reinstatement was only one of the factors relevant to the decision as to which basis of assessment was appropriate.

Gardner v Marsh & Parsons (1997)

On the basis of a survey carried out by the defendant, the claimants bought a long lease of a maisonette. A covenant in the lease provided that the landlord would rectify structural defects. A serious structural defect was later discovered which should have been identified by the defendants. The defendants were entitled to compensation on the basis of the difference between the price paid by the claimants and the market price of the property in its defective condition at the time of their purchase, even though the landlord remedied the defect.

IMI Cornelius (UK) Ltd v Bloor (1991)

The defendant erected a storage building for the claimant. The claimant transferred its interest in the property to a sister company, for the purposes of internal group administration. The claimant brought an action in relation to alleged defects. The court held that a claimant who has parted with his ownership or other interest loses the right to recover as damages the cost of repairs, but does not lose the right to recover for the diminution in value suffered at the date the breach occurred.

Birse Construction Ltd v Eastern Telegraph Company Ltd (2004)

The court refused any award of damages in circumstances where a substantial snagging list and other defects had been left unremedied in a building by the time it had been sold, and where there had been no diminution in value brought about by the existence of the defects. It was held that if a building owner disposes of property with defects attributable to some breach of duty by the defendant and for which the cost of reinstatement was the appropriate measure but does so without any reduction or loss on account of its condition then the loss that the law supposes is avoided and no damages are recoverable. In some cases it may be reasonable (or even proportionate) to award an amount so that the contractor does not get paid for what was not done (if it was not done at all, then either an appropriate contractual reduction in the price or a comparable award of damages should be made).

Barclays Bank plc v Fairclough Building Ltd (No 2) (1994)

The claimant's roof was rendered unsafe by power hose cleaning, requiring replacement. The court held that the evidence of the claimant's intention to effect replacement the following year was only necessary to show the reasonableness of the date upon which they claimed the work would be done. If the claimant took the damages and then decides not to do the work, accepting all the risk and detriment that involves, that was a matter for them.

Nordic Holdings Ltd v Mott Macdonald Ltd (2001)

The claimants failed to establish negligence in relation to advice given as to the kind of floor to construct in a warehouse. In any event, the court held that even if liability had been established the evidence did not support the view that the claimant would build suspended floors and accordingly the claimant would not have been entitled to recover the cost of doing so as part of their damages.

Jones v Stroud District Council (1986)

The claimant was unable to show that he had paid for remedial works carried out to his property to rectify defective foundations. The court allowed the claim, stating that if property belonging to a claimant has been damaged to an extent which is proved and the court is satisfied that the property has been or will be repaired, the court is not further concerned with the question whether the owner has had to pay for the repairs out of his own pocket or whether the funds have come from some other source.

Bristol and West Building Society v Christie (1996)

The recovery by a bank of insurance proceeds against a loss caused by a negligent valuer could not be taken into account when determining the damages recoverable.

Design 5 v Keniston Housing Association Ltd (1986)

The claimants sued for nearly £90,000 as fees for architectural services. The defendants were a registered housing association. The defendants served a counterclaim, alleging negligence and breach of contract by the claimants in respect of design, supervision and administration, claiming that those failures by the claimants caused increased expenditure. The claimants were unsuccessful in arguing that whether or not they had been at fault in the respects alleged in the counterclaim, and whether or not the costs of the schemes had thereby been increased, nonetheless the defendants had not suffered and would not suffer loss because they were entitled to receive from the Department of the Environment 'the actual cost' to them of the building schemes, regardless of any fault of the claimants.

9.6 THE DATE OF ASSESSMENT OF THE COST OF REPAIR

The date of assessment depends, in all the circumstances, upon when it is reasonable to have carried out the repairs.

East Ham Corp v Bernard Sunley (1966)

The defects were discovered more than two years after the final certificate. It was held that the cost of reinstatement should be assessed at the time when the defects were in fact discovered and put right, rather than the lesser cost of when the architect might have discovered them during the course of inspections. This is because it must have been within the contemplation of the parties that there might be defects in the building which were not discoverable by a reasonable examination in the defects liability period.

Dodd Properties (Kent) Ltd v Canterbury City Council (1980)

The claimants owned and occupied a garage which was damaged by building operations carried out in 1968 by the one of the defendants. When the action came to trial ten years later, the remedial works had not been carried out. The claims for cost of repair and business interruption were claimed as at 1978, which were about three times higher than at the date of the damage. It was held that where there was a material difference between the cost of repair at the date of the wrongful act and the cost when the repairs could, having regard to all the relevant circumstances, first reasonably have been undertaken, the damages were to be assessed by reference to the cost of repair at the latter time. It was considered that the reasonableness of the deferment was to be equated with a claimant's duty to mitigate his damage and a claimant was not obliged in mitigating his damage to do what he could not afford to do.

W M Cory & Son Ltd v Wingate Investments (London Colney) Ltd (1980)

In 1972, the defendants constructed a distribution centre for the claimants, who then took a lease of the premises. The contract had specified concrete hard-standings. The defendants had provided tarmacadam. The claimants were awarded the cost of replacing the tarmacadam with concrete. At the trial in 1980, the cost of this work was awarded at then current prices. The question of the date at which the cost of resurfacing the car park was to be assessed was considered an aspect of the duty to mitigate.

9.7 RECOVERY OF BOTH COST OF REPAIR AND DIMINUTION IN VALUE

If there is a residual 'blight' notwithstanding repair of the defective work, this is recoverable as well as the cost of repair.

Thomas v TA Phillips (Builders) Ltd and Taff Ely BC (1985)

Subsequent purchasers of a development claimed against the builders and the local authorities, who approved the plans damages caused by defective foundations which it was said amounted to an imminent danger to health or safety of the occupants. The claimants were awarded damages amounting to the cost of repairs together with £3,000 in respect of the loss in value of their respective dwellings in addition to the cost of remedial works.

Murphy v Brentwood DC (1991)

The Court of Appeal recognised that in some instances, even when all the necessary remedial works have been carried out successfully, a house may still be less attractive to some purchasers and building societies than a comparable, trouble-free house. However, this diminution in value will not normally be recoverable from the local authority because that additional loss is not to be regarded as caused by the local authority's breach of duty. That duty is to ensure that the house is built in accordance with the byelaws or regulations and not to protect the owner-occupier from financial loss caused by the mistrust or dislike which purchasers or building societies have for a repaired house. The Court of Appeal disapproved *Thomas v Phillips* (above) insofar as it suggested otherwise, but did not state that dual recovery would not be appropriate against the builder (rather than the local authority). This was not affected by the House of Lords decision.

Bigg v Howard Son & Gooch (1990)

In assessing a diminution in value (assessed by reference to the amount in fact paid and the amount the purchasers would have paid had they been aware of the defects), the court considered the cost of repair together with the existence of a small residual blight. The court then increased this sum on the basis that the reduction in price would be at least equal to the anticipated costs and fall in residual value, and probably rather more on the ground that people do not like having to spend money on doing a major operation to a house and not knowing what they may find when they do that major operation.

George Fischer Holdings Ltd v Multi Design Consultants Ltd (1998)

In relation to a claim arising out of roof defects and defective rainwater disposal, the claimant succeeding in establishing a claim for loss of value of £100,000 on the basis that even after completion of remedial works the property would not be worth as much as it would have been had there not been the defects for which the defendant was liable.

9.8 BETTERMENT

9.8.1 'New for old'

Generally, there is no discount for 'new for old' replacement of damaged or defective property.

Hollebone v Midhurst & Fernhurst Builders Ltd (1968)

In a case where there was a fire at the claimant's house due to defective building works, the defendant claimed a reduction in the cost of repair due to betterment. The court considered that whist it was true that the repair work had deferred the need for rewiring in the damaged part of the house for some 15 to 20 years – thus benefiting the claimants an amount assessed at £250 – the court decided that it would not be fair to the claimant to make such a deduction.

Harbutt's 'Plasticine' Ltd v Wayne Tank and Pump Co Ltd (1970)

The plaintiff's factory was completely destroyed by a fire which was the responsibility of the defendant. A new factory had to be built. The court decided that where a building was destroyed and the innocent party had no option but to rebuild a new one, the proper measure of damages was the cost of replacement. Where claimants acted reasonably to mitigate their loss, the defendants were not entitled to any allowance for any benefit to the plaintiffs from having a new factory in place of the old.

Imperial College of Science and Technology v Norman & Dawbarn (1986)

The architects negligently designed one of Imperial College's buildings. The design work was carried out in 1956 and the building was completed in 1968. By 1977 tiles fell from the roof in consequence of the negligent design. Remedial work consisting of replacement of the tiles was carried out in 1984. The tiling would have had to have been replaced after 30 years in any event. It was held that the college had to reclad the block if it were to continue effectively as before. The defendants were liable for the full cost of replacement.

Barclays Bank plc v Fairclough Building Ltd (No 2) (1994)

The claimant owned buildings, 30 years old, with roofs of corrugated asbestos cement sheeting. The roofs, which were not watertight, were negligently cleaned by power hosing and a slurry containing asbestos entered the building. The diminution in value was so great that it was accepted that replacement of the roof was reasonable mitigation. The claimant would have replaced the roof in 2015 anyway. The court held that it would be impossible to replace an ageing roof with a roof of a similar age (as it might with a car). No reduction for betterment was allowed.

Bacon v Cooper (Metals) Ltd (1982)

The plaintiff obtained from the defendant a fragmentiser fitted with a rotor. If properly maintained, the rotor had an average life of seven years. If broken, the rotor could only be replaced by a completely new one. The rotor was damaged beyond repair when it could have been used for a further three-and-three-quarter years, and the plaintiff's business came to a standstill.

The defendant bore the full cost of replacement of the rotor, not some proportion to take account of the likely replacement in the future.

Oswald v Countrywide Surveyors Ltd (1996)

The defendant surveyors had failed to report an infestation of death watch beetle. In assessing a diminution in value, the court considered the cost of remedial work as evidence of the difference in value. However, this cost was discounted so as not to ignore the fact that the claimants would end up with a building better than the one they had thought they were buying.

9.8.2 Betterment: building to a higher standard

If a higher specification is not necessary, a credit in respect of additional cost is allowed.

Richard Roberts v Douglas Smith Stimson (1988)

As the result of an architect's breaches of contract, the claimant had a defective tank and mixing room floor. Both parties' experts agreed as to the right methods of remedying the defects. The remedial works would only achieve what the claimant should have received under the contract. The court considered that if the only practicable method of overcoming the consequences of a defendant's breach of contract was to build to a higher standard than the contract had required, a claimant may recover the cost of building to that higher standard. If, however, a claimant, needing to carry out works because of a defendant's breach of contract, chooses to build to a higher standard than is strictly necessary, the courts will, unless the new works are so different as to break the chain of causation, award him the cost of the works less a credit to the defendant in respect of betterment. In this case there was no betterment for which the architects could obtain credit.

9.9 MITIGATION

In effecting rectification work in the light of defects, the innocent party is under a duty to act reasonably.

The burden of proof is upon the party seeking to show that the innocent party had acted unreasonably.

Lodge Holes Colliery Co Ltd v Wednesbury Corporation (1908)

Mine workings had caused subsidence of a highway which the local authority had restored to its former level at the 'great cost' of £400, when an equally suitable solution would have cost £65. The House of Lords held that since the authority had not considered at all whether or not they could properly have constructed the cheaper, but equally satisfactory, road the authority could only recover the amount which it would have cost them to have done so. It was considered that, in judging whether the claimant had acted reasonably, the court should be 'very indulgent and always bear in mind who is to blame'.

Hutchinson v Harris (1978)

The claimant successfully sued the defendant architect for, amongst other things, negligently certifying payment for defective work. The claimant was unable to recover lost rent on the property because she could have got on with letting these premises, but chose not to do so. The court considered that the claimant should have got the work completed by another builder.

Hospitals for Sick Children v McLoughlin & Harvey plc (1990)

In relation to defects within the new cardiac wing of the claimant hospital, it was reasonable to undertake extensive remedial work. Where works have been carried out, the court stated that it was not for the court to consider from scratch what should have been done and what costs should have been incurred. The claimant acted upon the advice of an expert, whose views were within the range of those which an ordinary competent expert would have adopted, and therefore the actual costs expended were recoverable.

Riverside Property Investments Ltd v Blackhawk Automotive (2004)

All other things being equal, under a building contract where proper remedial works can be carried out in one of two ways, the cheapest option will be appropriate.

9.10 THE BASIC PRINCIPLE: FAILURE TO IDENTIFY DEFECTS

If a valuer negligently fails to identify defects whilst valuing the property, the loss to the purchaser upon buying the property is not the cost of having the defects repaired, but the difference in value of the property with and without defects.

Philips v Ward (1956)

The claimant purchased a property for £25,000 in reliance on a negligent and inaccurate report by the defendant surveyor. After moving in, the claimant found that it would require an additional expenditure of £7,000 to put the property into the condition in which it had been described in the report. The market value of the property in its actual condition was, as at the date of purchase, £21,000. The proper measure of damages was £4,000, not the cost of repair. If, upon learning of the real condition of the house, the claimant had decided to leave and resell, he would probably have been entitled to recover from the defendant, in addition to the £4,000, his costs and expenses of moving in and moving out and of the resale. As, however, the claimant elected to stay after discovery of the defects, this point did not arise.

Watts v Morrow (1991)

The claimants bought a property for £177,500 in reliance on a building surveyor's report, which had failed to identify certain defects. The cost of the repairs which were carried out amounted to £33,961. The claimants' loss was assessed by reference not to the cost of these repairs, however, but by the difference between the value of the property as it was represented to be and its value in its true condition, namely £15,000.

9.10.1 The relevance of an increase in resale price

Hussey v Eels (1990)

The claimants, who purchased a bungalow in February 1984 in reliance upon negligent answers to pre-contract inquiries about subsidence, were entitled to recover £17,000, being the difference between the £53,250 they had paid in 1984 and its then market value. The Court of Appeal rejected the judge's conclusion that their gain on resale had wiped out their initial loss, on the basis that the claimants' resale of the land and bungalow was no part of a continuous transaction of which their purchase was the inception. In these circumstances it could not be said that the negligence which caused damage to the claimants had also caused whatever profit they had made on resale.

9.11 CONSEQUENTIAL LOSSES

Consequential losses in addition to the cost of repair or diminution in value will be awarded, appropriate to the basis of assessment. The costs may include damage caused by the defects and business interruption.

Bevan Investments Ltd v Blackhall & Struthers (1978)

The design of a speculative development, namely a recreation centre comprising a skating rink, squash courts and sauna facilities, was discovered to be defective during the course of construction. A new scheme was put forward, using as much as possible of what had already been built. However, at this time the company was unable to obtain sufficient finance to enable the project to be continued. The development did not proceed. The court held that the company had been deprived of the opportunity to trade and attempt to make a profit. It seemed probable that if the company had been able to trade some profit would have been earned and an assessment of £10,000 was made.

Tate & Lyle Distribution v GLC (1982)

The claimants claimed that they had expended managerial and supervisory resources in attending to the problems created by heavy deposits of silt formed in the River Thames, for which they alleged the defendant was liable. The court was satisfied that this head of damage could properly be claimed, and considered that there was evidence that managerial time was in fact expended on dealing with remedial measures. However, in the absence of any evidence about the extent to which this occurred, the court was not prepared to advance into an area of pure speculation and held that the claimants had failed to prove that any sum was due.

Raflatac Ltd v Eade (1999)

The claimants employed the defendant to replace its sprinkler system. In negligently carrying out the works, water flooded out and damaged large paper rolls in an adjoining store. In respect of additional labour costs incurred in cleaning up the flooded area and in selling the damaged stock, £657 was recovered, on the basis that but for having to do this work, those engaged on it would be doing other normal work in the claimant's organisation.

Rawlings v Rentokil Laboratories Ltd (1972)

The defendant was employed to install a damp-proof system. The damp-proof system failed and the claimant was entitled to recover, in addition to the difference between the value of the property but for the breach and the lower price the claimant in fact obtained, the cost of legal fees incurred in abortive attempts to sell the defective house.

Riverside Property Investments Ltd v Blackhawk Automotive (2004)

(The facts of this case are set out at 9.9 above.) A claim for managerial time allegedly spent on account of the defendant's default, failed because (amongst other reasons) there were no time records whatsoever to support the hours identified as having been expended over the relevant period.

Johnston v W H Brown Construction (Dundee) Ltd (1999)

The costs of the identification and notification of defects as part of the ordinary operation of a contractual procedure were not a head of loss ordinarily recoverable as damages at common law. Whilst there might be exceptional circumstances in which such costs might be recoverable, they would not be recoverable the costs had been incurred in the ordinary operation of the defects liability clause.

George Fischer Holdings Ltd v Multi Design Consultants Ltd (1998)

The claimant claimed as damages the costs of preparing a remedial scheme which, ultimately, the court did not adopt when deciding between rival remedial schemes at trial. The court considered that the cost of such preparatory work stands or falls with the remainder of the cost of the remedial scheme in question. Therefore, they were not recoverable as damages. However, the court stated that (notwithstanding the costs having been pleaded as damages), they might nevertheless fall to be considered as costs of the action subject to assessment in the usual way.

Amec Process and Energy Ltd v Stork Engineers & Contractors BV (2002)

Amec engaged its own personnel and agency staff to undertake much of the work involved in collecting, analysing and presenting the primary evidence and the supporting evidence the expert. These personnel also undertook much of the preparation of visual evidential aids such as isographs, histograms, graphs, bar charts, photographs, tables, as built programmes and overlays. In principle, the time charges involved in employing these personnel fall within each of these categories of *Civil Procedure Rules* 1998 (CPR), CPR 43.2(1)(a), which defines 'costs' as including 'fees, charges, disbursements, expenses, remuneration …'.

The reasonableness of the time and the rates is a matter for assessment.

Sisu Capital Fund Ltd v Tucker & Ors (2005)

Amec v Stork (above) was not followed. The court found that the costs that a litigant must bear of digging out his own factual material, through his own employees, to prove his own case are not recoverable. Even if outside experts had been introduced to carry out this work then the costs would not necessarily have been recoverable as a cost of the litigation.

9.12 DAMAGES FOR LOSS OF AMENITY, DISTRESS, ANXIETY AND INCONVENIENCE

Modest damages for discomfort and inconvenience will be allowed where there has been breach of a contract which was one to provide peace of mind or enjoyment.

Contracts whose purpose is purely commercial – where the plaintiff is merely seeking a profit out of the contract – cannot be treated in the same way as contracts which have non-commercial objectives.

Watts v Morrow (1991)

The claimants, who were husband and wife, purchased a property as a second home on reliance upon a survey which did not properly identify the extent of the defects. On appeal, the court considered that the proper approach is to fix a modest sum for the amount of physical discomfort endured having regard to the period of time over which it was endured. The period of physical discomfort caused by the carrying out of work extended over eight months. The award of £4,000 each for distress and inconvenience was reduced to £750 each.

Wallace v Manchester City Council (1998)

In a review of the authorities relating to the award of damages for distress, inconvenience and loss of amenity in cases of disrepair under the *Landlord and Tenant Act* 1985, the Court of Appeal considered there to be an unofficial tariff of damages of £2,750 per annum at the top, to £1,000 per annum at the bottom.

9.12.1 Table of authorities

The following is a table of authorities dealing with distress and inconvenience damages awards. The table updates the helpful table appearing in Kim Franklin's article at (1992) 8 Const LJ 318 which stopped with *Watts v Morrow* in 1991. The table also gives approximate updated values based upon RPI.

Case	Date	Citation	Judge	Period	Description	Quantum	2006 prices
Heatley v William H Brown	1991	EGCS 115	HHJ Bowsher QC	Not known	Property structurally unsound. Cannot use bathroom inside.	£4,500	£6,684
Henley v Cloke	1991	37 EG 145	HHJ Thane Forbes	5 months	Front bay distorted and settlement throughout.	£2,000	£2,970
Appleton v Murten	1993	CLY 1386	DJ Foster	2 years	Windows admitted draughts and leaks, water down the side of the house. Suffering 'not great'.	£400	£561
Butcher v Perkins	1994	10 Const LJ 67	Brandt J	4 years	Remedial works to cracking caused by tree roots in foundations. During work either will move away or live with the work.	£1,200	£1,782
Makan v British Gas	1994	CLY 1466	DJ Bradfield	9 months	Ceiling collapsed in living room and bathroom, leaving plaster and debris and dust, and a hole in ceiling.	£2,000	£2,737
Beaver v Pennine Building Contractors	1994	CLY 1762	DJ Lingard	3 weeks	Negligent survey, house infested. Prop in living room holding ceiling up, removal of all non-essential possessions, living on convenience food; 'appalling problems'.	£2,000	£2,737
Credit Suisse v Beegas Nommees Ltd	1994	11 EG 151	Lindsay J	2 years	Leaking water from defective cladding. Disturbance and inconvenience to staff and customers.	£40,000	£59,659

Case	Date	Citation	Judge	Period	Description	Quantum	2006 prices
Lea v North West Water Ltd	1994	11 Const LJ 465	HHJ Mackay	1 year	Substantial subsidence caused significant degree of upset and dislocation, removal from home.	£4,500	£6,159
Newham LBC v Hewitt	1995	CLY 15663	Recorder White	4 years	Radiators in the bathroom, living room and hall defective and not working.	£850pa	£1,126pa
Lally v Whitely	1995	CLY 1852	HHJ Downey	8 weeks	Vacation of premises during remedial work.	£500	£662
Hannant and Curran v Harrison	1995	CLY 1562	Mr Recorder Hield	6 months	Substantial interference to use of property. Sleeping in sitting room and having to change in small bathroom.	£1,000	£1,325
Ezekial v McDade	1995	47 EG 150	Court of Appeal	Not known	Heavy concrete purlin discovered mispositioned in roof. Plaintiff depressed at diminution in value, was dismissed from work.	£4,000 (reduced from £6,000 on appeal)	£5,299 (reduced from £7,948)
Lessey v Lambeth LBC	1995	CLY 1573	Recorder Susman	12 years	12 people in house. 1983–85: Water penetration, top floor uninhabitable, basement damp. Buildings causing significant disruption. 1987–95: Continuing problems, kitchen damp and unusable.	1983–85; 1987–95 £1,500pa 1986–87 £4,000pa	1983–85; 1987–95 £1,987pa 1986–87 £5,299pa
Lewin v Brent LB	1995	CLY 1574	HHJ Diamond QC	2 years	Manholes overflowing with sewage onto lawn.	£1,000	£1,325

Case	Date	Citation	Judge	Period	Description	Quantum	2006 prices
Brown v West Midlands Patio Doors Ltd	1997	CLY 933	HHJ McEvoy QC	2 years	Work to windows, 'appalling'. Broken glass, fitted incorrectly, house left dirty after work.	£1,500	£1,879
Sealey v Hammersmith & Fulham LBC	1997	CLY 2641	HHJ Ryland	3 years	Continual difficulties with defective boiler. 3 weeks to replace, during which no hot water. Bath and toilet removed for 1 week.	£1400 (plus £100 for each of 4 children)	£1,754 (plus £125 for each of 4 children)
Glynn v Thames Water Utilities Ltd	1997	CLY 4965	HHJ Ryland	1 year	Extensive flood caused living on the top floor for 3 months, vacating for 3 months and then 6 months' further disruption.	£1,600	£2,004
Richardson v Quercus	1997	SCLR 815	JF Wheatley QC	Not known	Serious damage to property. Move out during remedial building and redecoration works.	£2,000	£2,505
Piatkus v Harris	1997	CLY 1747	HHJ Maher	18 months	Defective electrical work, lights flashing on and off, transformers blowing.	£200	£251
Brydon v Islington BC	1997	CLY 1754	HHJ Gibson	4 years	Leak in pantry, walls severely stained, kept bucket to catch leak which sometimes overflowed. 'Considerable inconvenience' during remedial works.	£2,250	£2,818

Case	Date	Citation	Judge	Period	Description	Quantum	2006 prices
Holmes v Lambeth LBC	1997	CLY 2643	DJ Gittens	2 years	Penetrating damp due to defects in rainwater installation. Windows not open. 'Severe disruption' during remedial work, vacating for 4 weeks.	£2,000	£2,505
Switzer v Law	1998	CLY 3624	Judge Morgan	8 years	Condensation and damp, considerable disruption during remedial works.	£5,500	£6,669
Enus v Tower Hamlets LBC	1998	CLY 2987	Recorder Haines	Not known	Severe mould growth, dampness and excessive condensation.	£1,250pa	£1,516pa
Wallace v Manchester City Council	1998	30 HLR 1111	Court of Appeal	N/A	The amounts awarded so as to arrive at current values indicate an unofficial tariff of damages for discomfort and inconvenience of £2,750pa at the top to £1,000pa at the bottom.	As stated	£3,334 at the top to £1,213 at the bottom
Welsh v MacBryde Homes plc	1999	CLY 788	Recorder Hernandez	4 years 8 months	Defective joists; first floor deflected excessively and was extremely noisy. Sleep disturbance and loss of enjoyment.	£4,750	£5,760
Mitchell v Durham	1999	CLY 1375	DJ Douce	2 years	Defective double glazing. 'Appalling state'. Mrs M particularly affected, thought home ruined and was in despair.	Mrs: £1,000 Mr: £500	Mrs: £1,184 Mr: £592
Ogefere v Islington LBC	1999	CLY 1391	DJ Southcombe	2.5 years	Dampness and condensation.	£3,450	£4,083
Mulligan v Halton	1999	CLY 3674	DJ Bennett	1.5 years	Penetrating dampness, defective windows, loose and dangerous electrical sockets, draughts.	£2,750	£3,254

Case	Date	Citation	Judge	Period	Description	Quantum	2006 prices
Hoadley v Edwards	2001	EGCS 46		3 years	Defective plumbing, windows, wall ties.	£5,000	£5,652
Farley v Skinner	2002	1 BLR 1	House of Lords	N/A	Claimant suffered disturbance from aircraft noise.	£10,000	£11,159
Gemma v Gimson	2004	CILL 2143	HHJ Thornton QC	90 weeks	Hostile builders (who lived next door to the claimants).	£4,500 per adult (£50/wk) £1,000 for children Total £10,000	£4,753 per adult (£53/wk) £1,056 for children Total £10,562

Index

The *Case in Point* series

The *Case in Point* series is a popular set of concise practical guides to legal issues in land, property and construction. Written for the property professional, they get straight to the key issues in a refreshingly jargon-free style.

Areas covered:

Negligence in Valuation and Surveys
Stock code: 6388
Published: December 2002

Party Walls
Stock code: 7269
Published: May 2004

Service Charges
Stock code: 7272
Published: June 2004

Estate Agency
Stock code: 7472
Published: July 2004

Rent Review
Stock code: 8531
Published: May 2005

Expert Witness
Stock code: 8842
Published: August 2005

Lease Renewal
Stock code: 8711
Published: August 2005

VAT in Property and Construction
Stock code: 8840
Published: September 2005

Construction Adjudication
Stock code: 9040
Published: October 2005

Dilapidations
Stock code: 9113
Published: January 2006

Planning Control
Stock code: 9391
Published: April 2006

If you would like to be kept informed when new *Case in Point* titles are published, please e-mail **rbmarketing@rics.org.uk**

All RICS Books titles can be ordered direct by:

☎   Telephoning 0870 333 1600 (Option 3)

🖱   Online at www.ricsbooks.com

📠   E-mail mailorder@rics.org.uk